EXTREME NAZARENE

Present Day Saints and Soldiers

Adam P. Childress

Senior Pastor of Family Worship Las Vegas

PublishAmerica Baltimore

ISBN: 1-4241-9726-0 PUBLISHED BY PUBLISHAMERICA, LLLP
www.publishamerica.com
Baltimore

Printed in the United States of America.

This book is dedicated to the father of my faith. I am so grateful for the love, discipline, and mentorship you have poured into my life. I can still hear your voice preaching and teaching in your unique manner. You are one of a kind. Now, I can continue to share your inspiration with the whole world. This harvest began with you. You are a mighty man of God, the father of my faith, Pastor Paul Palmer.

Table of Contents

Introduction i
Chapter 1: Boot Camp.. 1
   A. Basic Training: Become Transformed 1
   B. Proper Etiquette.. 5
   C. March in Cadence 8
   D. Balance and Order.. 10
   E. Physical Fitness 17
   F. Grade and Rank.. 19
   G. Uniform 23
   H. Weapons Qualification 29
   I. Wisdom and Discipline 34
   J. Chow Time... 36
   K. Preventative Maintenance Checks and Services 39
   L. The Nazarene dual Pledge of Allegiance 41
   M. Dual Citizenship... 44
Chapter 2: Combat Readiness.. 47
   A. Soldier of Amor 47
   B. Soldier of Velvet... 49
   C. Soldier of Steel... 51
   D. Tour of Duty... 55
   E. Lock and Load.. 61
   F. Prisoner of Christ Jesus 65
   G. Red, White and Blue 67
Chapter 3: Battlefield Operations 71
   A. Knowing the Terrain.. 71
   B. Forward Observer... 77
   C. Posturing Valor 79
   D. PTSD (Post Traumatic Stress Disorder).............. 83
   E. Knowing the Objective... 89
   F. Communications, Command and Control of 92
Chapter 4: My Testimony.. 97
Chapter 5: Quantum Faith 106

Example of Church Structure for the United Saint Nazarene Corp.. 113
Introduction to the EXTREME NAZARENE "United Saints Nazarene Corp.".. 115
    What is a Nazarene? 117
    Who can be a Nazarene? 118
        Nazarene Company Foundation 118
        Nazarene Vision 118
Book and Scripture References 121
Acknowledgments 125

Introduction

"Postponed obedience is disobedience" (Unknown).

"The wishbone will never replace the backbone" (Will Henry).

"The natural man must know in order to believe; the spiritual man must believe in order to know" (A.W. Tozer).

For some time, the Lord has put it on my heart to write a book that spoke to a Christian about living the life of a Christian soldier. The reality of this book is stunning and heroic. I want to share a concept with everyone who is reading this information. As a people of God almighty, we have dual citizenship in this life: our present condition and our future condition in Christ. We have to conquer our flesh and stand righteous before the world and our fellow soldiers. The aim of this book is to assist us in Christian soldiering, to live life in the second coming and not be left behind. It is Combat Faith that leads us to a reckless abandonment of ourselves and press forcefully toward the enemy's camp to take back the ground we are swiftly losing in this present age. Darkness is all around us. We are surrounded (in the spiritual realm) and with ample supplies. However, we have yet to learn to tap into the resource. We are trapped into thinking we are alone and with limited resources. As the smoke clears and with the sound of mortar still ringing in your ears, shadows of the walking wounded cast their broken images. As you wipe clear the sting of smoke burning your eyes, waves of bleeding bodies are all over the place, soldiers falling to fatal wounds. Night casts its blanket of blindness upon you. No reinforcement. No hope in sight. Sulfur and gunpowder are in your nostrils. Screaming soldiers are looking for direction, most shell-shocked and frightened out of their minds. You are in charge of leading them to safety. What do you do? Who do you ask? How are you going to survive? Where is it all going to come from, and who is going to rescue you now? These questions are typical and feared among those faced with overwhelming odds such as these. It is my hope to take some examples from God's word and laterally transform them into a common military language and understanding for those with a military mind. As a Christian soldier, we have a duty to preserve our Christian heritage and our country's principles! "Endure hardship with us like a good soldier. No one serving as a soldier gets involved in civilian affairs-he wants to please his commanding officer" (2 Timothy 2:3). Our faith begins to separate our priorities, defining who we are and our responsibilities in every arena of life. We must involve ourselves in the affairs of this world as we have been assigned a duty station and not a permanent residence. We have been assigned to station earth, country, state, city, and address. Our awesome high God (Commander and Chief) has assigned us. He has chosen our skin color, sex, abilities, nationalities, and limitations. As soldiers, we are dedicated to the "Great Commission." We are to reach out to this lost and dying world for Christ.

This love is Christ's battlefield. We are the Christian soldiers occupying the territories of the lost souls in captivity, rescuing fallen Christian fellow soldiers, wounded in combat or simply AWOL (Backsliders). Circumstances do not define life. We define life and circumvent the moment for Christ. Victory has been declared and paid for by Christ. We must not lose our ground in the smoke screens of life's warfare. Let us prepare for warfare as we learn to put on the armor of Christ and take charge of every moment of every day. This commentary is to help you see a vision of who we could be in Christ's army if all of us understood what it meant to have a universal uniform to our faith. When this world sees your faith, does it match anyone else? Why are we all so different? We should all look the same. We all are the image of Christ and the glory of God. We should be identical in faith, heart, and living posture.

Chapter 1: Boot Camp

A. Basic Training: Become Transformed

"Other books were given for our information; the bible was given for our transformation" (Unknown).

"We should all be concerned with the future, because we will have to spend the rest of our lives there" (Charles Kettering).

"The calm that puts us to sleep may be more deadly than the storm that keeps us awake" (Unknown).

"Do not conform any longer to the patterns of this world, but be transformed by the renewing of your mind. Then will you be able to test and approve what God's will is-his good, pleasing and perfect will" (Romans 12:2). Let us capture one sentence at a time. To be transformed by the renewing of your mind is to clean up your thought life. Let us make it as simple as possible. Three ways to change our stinky thinking: prayer and fasting, reading the Bible and studying the stories, and memorizing scripture. As a young believer or a mature believer, you cannot exhaust the treasures and knowledge of God's everlasting word. Prayer opens up our communication with our commander on high. Oftentimes, we need to submit to His grace for understanding, hope, direction, and power in circumstances beyond our control. Other times, simply to say hello and sit in His mighty presence and dream of eternity. This mindset helps us to know we are not in control. He is; He sees the bigger picture. The key to learning who you are is to read the word and study every word you read. Cross-reference every subject, issue, and story. Ask yourself how does this relate to me as a soldier in Christ's command? How can I apply this lesson to myself? How can you use what you have just learned to further the command of God? Go back in time. Stand where the apostles stood and feel the scenery. Act out the part in your heart. Finally, repetition is the key to memorization, and memorization of scripture is the key to learning your military Christian history and duty. In addition, your new thought life changes and your mind is becoming Holy. With more knowledge comes more responsibility; with more responsibility comes more authority, and spiritual combat is sure to follow. Your mind is the battle zone, and your thoughts are your radar scanner. Your eyes scope the terrain, and your ears listen to the sphere of influence picked up on your radar. What is your next move? Think about it.

That move would be to go back to your basic training (prayer, reading, and memorizing). It is crucial to have a Christian combat buddy to share your struggles, battles, and triumphs. Camaraderie is well-known among military personnel and veterans. A comradeship is found through shared interest and a common occupation of service. I have spent many hours toiling, overexpressing the commonality of an "esprit de corps" among men in the church, in their homes, neighbors, businesses, and places of work. Your combat buddy is someone you can share the most confident and private issues of the heart. This is sensitive information, on a need-to-know basis only; top secret clearance. A person in the military never forgets his or her military bearing. Christian soldiers are held to an even higher standard. Keeping the confidence of our fellow comrade's heart is crucial to healing and spiritual growth. As for military personnel, whether they are in military clothes or not, they are in military posture, never forgetting who they are and whom they are in service to. As a Christian soldier, we should never forget whom we serve and to soldier Christian bearing with integrity and enthusiasm. Esprit de corps is a French phrase for having a spirit of enthusiastic devotion to and support of the common goals of the group. Men and women, we need a Godly esprit de corps in the church today! We need to show boys and girls how to be Godly young men and women. We need to teach our young men and women how to be mature people of God. This is how we will become Christian personnel, and teach our Christian personnel to never forget their Christian bearing, whether in our church clothes or in our "civies."

We need to be soldiers and Christians at all times, no half-stepping. As Nazarenes, we are soldiers in military service to Christ, our Commander and Chief. The yearning was so strong to get this common bond between Christian brothers that I approached my mentor and men's leader, Pastor Mike Richardson, and asked him if I could try an experiment with the men in our group. I told him, I was hoping that the theory that military men do not forget their basic military bearing and basic training was true. He agreed to allow me the trial run. On the night of our meeting, we put it to test. We agreed to see a show of hands for those men who were in service or had served in the armed forces. I wanted to have them fall into formation. (Formation is the gathering of an element of men grouped together in dress right, dress manner.) Pastor Mike called me forward. I jumped to my feet and, with a military command voice, sounded off by saying, "On your feet!" These men transformed into military bearing instantly. I explained to the men with that familiar tone and bark, "You will fall out of your groups and fall into my right on my command!" I yelled, "Fall out and fall in as directed!"

I could not believe my eyes. Men of every age running swiftly to formation, orderly, yet with military readiness and a basic understanding of the directive given. Immediately, these men began to perform the basic dress right, dress procedure. I was wide-eyed and proudly shocked with excitement. They were already working side by side in seconds. They were poised in position and prepared for their next command. They waited with bated breath. There was complete silence as I inspected my newly formed motley Christian personnel. Hand extended forward, eyes looking to the right of every man with the right arm extended, barely touching his fellow soldier. I was elated and very satisfied to see such precision. I called out my next command, "Arms downward, move!" Arms dropped and I was looking into the eyes of at least seventy-five outstanding men who had never been called to a formation such as this. I was moved and privileged to be in command. As I called out ten different commands, the men became smoother and more mechanical. They executed with a degree of urgency and military proficiency. After an excellent performance, I did an about-face to face the men's group to see their reaction. The men in our group sat in utter amazement.

After the huge applause, Pastor Mike explained that no one person was contacted before this moment, and no one was privy to the formation. After the pastor released the men back to me, no one broke formation until I had officially dismissed them. They were proud to be commanded and to serve together in the "esprit de corps" of Christ. I found the high-fives, hugs, handshakes, and pats on the back to be as exciting as the entire drill. These men had found themselves working together as a whole. No issues arose as they became one unit and of one accord. They became comrades instantly, and there was a high level of "esprit de corps." They had a common bond due to a similar understanding of what it takes to be many parts in one complete unit. These men experienced an energy level which sparked the very basic standard operating procedures learned as soldiers through drill and practice as a uniform body. Some of these good men had not been called to a formation in over thirty years. The comments were incredible, to say the least. Men were saying they had walked back to their small groups, and tears filled their eyes. Others were challenged to keep good old military memories alive and contacted old friends. Others were happy to be experiencing old familiar feelings and being commanded again. I believe we need to transform (impact) this quality of camaraderie by learning basic Christian soldiering and applying its principles as Nazarene soldiers.

B. Proper Etiquette

"One of our greatest problems is not the mistakes we make in life, but that we fail to learn from them. If one can come up with creative new mistakes, that's something else, but if we make the same ones over and over, we're not learning" (Unknown).

"God creates out of nothing. Therefore, until a man is nothing, God makes nothing out of him" (Martin Luther).

"Temptations, unlike opportunities, will always give you many second chances" (Unknown).

Our code of ethics begins with understanding authority. Hebrews shines a bright light in the direction of truth when speaking about authority. It says, "Obey your leaders and submit to their authority. They keep watch over you as men who must give an account. Obey them so that their work will be a joy, not a burden, for that would be of no advantage to you" (Hebrews 13:17).

My study bible goes on to clarify this verse as follows, "Dictatorial leadership is not condoned by this command, but respect for authority, orderliness, and discipline in the church are taught throughout the new testament" (Concordia self-study bible commentary). Authority, orderliness and discipline are military etiquettes due upon your oath to serve and defend America. Will you serve and defend our faith? Have you made an oath to God to stand firm in the truth of His word and the work of His grace on the cross for our sins? If you have, then show how much you love our Holy Commander and Chief by obeying His command. I have found out that the only way to render respect to anyone is to honor Christ in him first and then respect the man's position and/or title.

Oftentimes, a man's character may be unknown to you. It is your duty not to judge him but to honor Christ in him. Uniformity of heart. Respect will only be accomplished through rendering it in submission through authority as a lifestyle. We are lacking a great deal of authority and submission to authority in our God and the local church. As Nazarenes, we have a clear assignment. We need to lead the way, show discipline, model order and respect for authority, and walk in authority as we develop into Christian soldiers, real Nazarene. Military soldiers are taught to stand in the position of attention when addressed by an officer. When a person of authority is speaking to us, we will show the utmost respect and pay close attention to detail. We will not fidget or be unconcerned about the communication being disseminated. We are soldiers first and friends last. In battle, we are brothers. As soldiers, we do not mistake friendship with someone of authority for our personal means and gains. This is clearly a misuse of Christian military bearing. We also call this spiritual amnesia. We must remember who we are and whom we serve first. We must keep a balanced perspective of Christian soldiering and a deep sense of honor toward our leaders. Soon, you will be leading at a higher call and you will remember what it felt like giving honor to whom honor is due. Let me give you a good example: when I or my fellow soldiers call our pastors, we do not leave messages on voice mail or recordings calling them by their first name. We do not speak to them on an intercom and assume they are alone. In public, we especially keep our military bearing and act like men of God, never taking advantage of our personal relationship with our pastor or leader. As far as anyone else knows around you, you are a "regular joe," just like everyone else. No one should detect your friendship; it may be mutually deeper than that of those you may be associating with at the time.

Our pastor's first name is "Pastor," and that is all anyone needs to know about your friendship. When you are one-on-one (never a male with female), what you call your pastor is yours and his mutual appreciation as to the level of familiarity, friendship, and trust. Maturity comes through a time-tested and proven ability to be historically and repetitiously reliable. "Of all things granted by wisdom, none is greater or better than friendship" (Pietro Aretino). Our etiquette distinguished us from the world at large. We say, "Yes, sir" and "Yes, ma'am." "Can I help you across the street, ma'am?" We stand up and make a difference for the defenseless; it is the difference we are to make. Mat 8:5-13 Gives us a great understanding of the principles of authority. The one with authority does not need to be present to accomplish the task. Orders may be carried out by others, even at a distance. To read that Jesus was astonished (to be surprised or amazed), this soldier understood his position in the chain of authority and understood the magnitude of his request. Simply the mere command of Jesus' voice would instantly authorize complete healing to his young servant. He (the centurion) believed Christ to be his superior without question. Jesus said, "I have not found anyone in Israel with such great faith." Faith such as this reproduces immediate results, and the servant was healed at that very hour. Our faith has everything to do with ushering righteous results as to whatever we are praying to be accomplished. Remember, we do not need to have Christ walk into our place of residence to acquire our request. We need to believe His power is just as great out of our sight and reach. Jesus said, "You did not choose me, but I chose you and appointed you to go and bear fruit. Fruit that will last. Then the father will give you whatever you ask in my name" (John15:16). Producing fruit which shows the evidence of our faith and asking, in faith, is our hope through our trust in Christ. We trust because we are under His authority as was the centurion.

C. March in Cadence

"All that is necessary for the triumph of evil is for good men to do nothing" (Edmond Burke).

"Some people dream of worthy accomplishments while others stay awake and do them" (Unknown).

"What is the greatest thought that can occupy a man's mind?" He replied,

"His accountability to GOD" (Daniel Webster).

Cadence is defined as "The beat, rate, or measure of any rhythmic movement." As a Nazarene soldier, you are truly marching to a different beat. I am sure you have seen a parade marching down the avenue, and someone happened to be out of step. Unfortunately, it makes everyone else behind that person feel awkward and uncomfortable. You become a distraction, and those behind you lose track or start to break their concentration on the leader of the march. The leader calls out a new command. You are out in no-man's land. You miss the command and are going in the wrong direction.

Let me confess now. It was not a parade down the avenue, and I am really describing a time when I was in boot camp. We were in the blue phase (the last two weeks of boot camp). We were at a drill march competition, and the drill sergeants were grading sharply. They were looking for attention to detail, dress right dress, uniformity, teamwork, proper execution of commands, personnel sound off, and preparedness. Our platoon (made of two or more squads) was the last to march, and I was nervous. Why? You see, I have a left and right malfunction when commanded to go left or right. For some reason, my mind, once in a while, reverses signals, and I will unintentionally go in the opposite direction. Crazy, but true. My father gave me some good advice. He said, "Carry a rock in your left hand. This will help you when your mind fails."

I was nervous and really anxious. I stepped to the right when I should have stepped to the left. I walked straight up to the drill sergeant who was grading. I could have fainted and totally lost my mind, like a psycho! But I prayed, jumped back in line, and no one saw me. We happened to win the drill competition, and I made it unscathed. (Only God is capable of such a cover up!) Next to be addressed is the "Spirit of Unity through the bond of peace" (Ephesians 4:3). How long will it take? "Until we all reach unity of faith and the knowledge of the Son of God, and become mature, attaining to the whole measure of the fullness of Christ" (Ephesians 4:13). Now, that is a very tall order. We are to embrace the ideals of Christ's teaching as a lifestyle unto death unless we attain perfection. No, no one has. However, this does imply faithfulness and uprightness in our daily walk to perfection, continually, with repetition. As a Nazarene, we demonstrate true piousness toward our God, family, church, and country; not a religious demeanor, but a healthy posturing of kingdom soldiers, a Nazarene! When you see a United Saints Nazarene soldier in America and compare them to one in Germany, they should act and look identical. If fast food can do it, so can we! Dress right dress and thirty inches all around. You heard me, now just do it! We must all act and look like Christ internationally and universally.

D. Balance and Order

"Far better it is to dare mighty things, to win glorious triumphs, even though checkered by failure, then to take rank with those poor spirits who neither enjoy much nor suffer much because they live in the gray twilight that knows neither victory nor defeat" (Teddy Roosevelt).

"If I rest, I rust" (Martin Luther).

"God enters by a private door into every individual" (Ralph Waldo Emerson).

The beginning of a new life in Christ will be the breaking down and putting off basic concepts and perceptions of personal strengths and weaknesses. Our thought life has everything to do with influencing our soul and others. To save our souls, we must first recognize our sole need for Christ's sacrifice to save our souls. I must caution you, if you are not a Christian, the following words may influence the rest of your life. As we, by faith, receive Jesus as our Savior, we believe we have died with Christ and our souls have been resurrected with Christ (Rom 6:8). Confess our sins and repent of our sinful ways and lifestyle, and our Supreme Commander and Chief becomes our blessed Savior. (Please note: If you read this passage and declare you are self-cleaned by the blood of Christ, congratulations! You are a soldier of Christ Jesus! Be sure to tell the nearest Christian you know. Buy a bible and start reading, memorizing and praying!)

Furthermore, our old thinking has died, and we now think with the mind of Christ (Col 2:20). Soldiering Christianity is not a matter of chance but a matter of choice. We choose to follow Christ as a lifestyle and set our minds on spiritual matters. Our lives are hidden in Christ (Col 3:3).

We put to death our earthly nature and rid ourselves of fleshly depravity. We speak the truth, hope, and love because we are soldiers of the cross. Daily we are renewing our mind in the knowledge of our creator. The father of my faith, Pastor Paul Palmer, taught me to rehearse the consequences of sin constantly. As a Nazarene, we must practice practical ways to guard against impurity. We must be consistent in our communion with God. Appropriate by faith our deliverance from sin. Be truthfully accountable to a pastor or mature friend (you know, like your combat buddy). If you are married, keep communication, authority, and romance a priority in your marriage. Be sure to break off any associations where you are likely to be tempted. You must be honest with yourself and with God. Recognize vulnerable areas. Remember, the enemy maximizes the pleasure and minimizes the consequence! Be ready, in and out of season. Having an attitude of grace to run the race full speed ahead. No slack, soldier, no slack! Keep your eyes on the target. Keep your mind on the objective, which would be the heavenly light of Christ. Keep moving!

"Forget what is behind and strain toward what is ahead" (Philippians 3:13). You were taught, with regard to your former way of life, to put off your old self, which is being corrupted by its deceitful desires, to be made new in the attitude of your minds, and to put on the new self, created to be like God in true righteousness and holiness" (Ephesians 4:22-24). Pastor Paul Palmer taught that the pitfalls for us men can be found in position, prosperity, and purity. The world exploits position in our social class. Dictates wealth as a means of becoming a status quo through prosperity. Never mind moral aptitude. Sleep with whom you wish; you are the big shot. Purity is for the common poor who cannot afford to sin. "Whatever is true, whatever is noble, whatever is right, whatever is pure, whatever is lovely, whatever is admirable—if anything is excellent or praiseworthy-think of these things" (Philippians 4:8).

This is worthy of repeating: as for our relationship with God, intimacy requires holiness; holiness requires humility; humility requires teachableness; teachableness requires thankfulness; thankfulness requires a listening ear! Sow a thought, reap an act; sow an act, reap a habit; sow a habit and reap a character; sow a character and reap a destiny! Is it possible to change and live a godly life? But I am weak and cannot do it on my own, you say?

Christ is quoted as saying, "My grace is sufficient for you, for

My power is made perfect in [your] weakness [Emphases added] (2 Corinthians 12:9). While acknowledging we sinners are saved by grace, through faith in Christ Jesus, He is now our Supreme Commander and Chief. As soldiers of the cross, we are on duty twenty-four hours a day, seven days a week. Our duty begins at home (I Tim 3:5). If you are single, you have a giant task. The world has endless enticements. Standing firm, pure, and accountable in Christ. This is your sole mission. Purity and innocence will be your anthem.

Remember to rehearse the consequence of sin. Recognize the pitfalls. Watch what comes to your mind.

Keep your thoughts heroic. "You are the light of the world. A city on a hill cannot be hidden" (Matthew 5:14). What is God's will for our lives? Her it is, "If you love me, you will obey me" (John 14:15). Love is always linked with obedience. Obedience is always linked with God's will and our destiny. We must remain in Him, read the following in (Jn 15:1-11). As you read God's word, you can see God's will clearly! Obey the laws of man and God. Your opinion is not required; your obedience is. If you are married, your attention is divided and your task becomes an act of pure finesse. This act is the artful strategy of balance and order. The order of created man is as follows: "Now I want you to realize that the head of every man is Christ, and the head of the woman is man, and the head of Christ is God" (1 Cor 11:3). Here's a saying worthy of repeating, a man sets the tone in the relationship to his wife. A wife sets the tone in the home in her relationship with the children, animals, and neighbors. Jesus sets the tone in our relationship with our Father in heaven. Husbands, you are ultimately responsible for your family. You are the authority in your home and this responsibility does weigh upon you. Those of you who are or have been in the armed forces understand the order of the military. Combat experienced personnel have been at one time leading or have been led into battle. As a leader you are the point man, and every aspect of the mission weighs on your ability to recognize all battle variables. Predict enemy travel, distance, approach, avenues of attack, elements of attack, weaponry, incoming rounds, modes of travel, headcounts, medical treatments, and tactics upon tactics. This is a very small picture. The variables are endless. Let us envision a similar battle zone with the enemy coming in your direction though you have not detected their exact coordinates, you decided to move forward. Something in the scenario has changed. There's something different about the patrol? Author Steve Farrar said it best in his excellent book, "Point Man."

"You look over your shoulder to see your wife and your children following behind. Your little girl is trying to choke back the tears, and your little boy is trying to act brave. Your wife is holding the baby and trying to keep him quiet. On this patrol, you do not want to engage the enemy, you want to avoid him. What would you be feeling under such conditions? The survival of each member of your family and its survival as a whole would be completely dependent upon your ability to lead through the maze of possible ambushes, unseen booby traps, invisible snipers, and all the extraordinary hazards of combat. Gentleman, this is no imaginary situation. It is reality. If you are a husband/father, then you are in a war. War has been declared upon the family, on your family and mine. LEADING A FAMILY THROUGH THE CHAOS OF AMERICAN CULTURE IS LIKE LEADING A SMALL PATROL THROUGH ENEMY-OCCUPIED TERRITORY. And the casualties in this war are as real as the names etched on the Vietnam Memorial."

If you ask yourself the same question you have just read, what would be your answer? Our focus in this chapter is to deal with the reality of this present darkness. Keeping the balance and order of Christianity a priority in your marriage, family, business, neighborhood, church, nation, and universe practical. A practical application of balance and order is to model submission, respect, and honor to our Savior, family, community, officials, governing authorities, and rulers (Rom 13:1-7). This attitude must become our basic instinct. Unfortunately, there are too many spiritually disabled Christians stuck at home under a vicious lie from the enemy. Sometimes, they get enough courage to go to church. Others want to be "Christers" (Christmas and Easter attenders, as our pastor would say). Our churches have adopted and gone to great lengths to prepare messages. Churches have enlarged hallways. They have put up handrails and installed ramps to provide for the many spiritually disabled Christians. Instead, we ought to be going door to door and providing spiritual rehabilitating therapy called the love of Christ. The warmth of fellowship our communities desperately need. We need not be judging them on how they look, sound, smell, talk, and act. We are the missionaries and evangelists of our streets and homes. We need to win the hearts of all our neighborhoods, cities, and states for Christ. We must be the future, or we will have no future. I have found that even when things do not make sense, just keep doing what is right, and God will reveal His plan through you. Sometimes it may be that God is growing you to maturity in an area of your life that you need discipline in. Just stand your ground and you will see that God will turn it for His good (yours too). When I was a private in the army, I was working as a cook. If you did not know, a cook was not a glamourous title or job. My NCO (noncommissioned officer) had elected me to do most of the repairs on our MKT (mobile kitchen trailer). It did not bother me right away. I was the only one out of seven other cooks in our platoon (unit of soldiers) to have to report to the motor pool to repair our equipment. As time passed (two years), I had been reading Romans 12:9 and 13:1-7 The words I read turned my discouragement into hope and love. I realized as I obeyed my NCO, I was fulfilling God's call as a believer. I kept my spiritual fervor and blessed my NCO. As the third year zipped by, I was also a sharp and able specialist (technical personnel). I had also represented our battalion (two or more batteries, there were five batteries) in Cook of the Quarter competitions. The Lord's favor was upon me. I had won six board competitions in a row. I truly believe because I had obeyed and submitted, God elevated me. I became an NCO in three in a half years. I was an NCO who knew every aspect of the job because I was made to do it. What my NCO meant for bad, God turned it for my good. I could have rebelled in my heart. I could have had an attitude when I was suffering. I chose to persevere. I did have moments when I battled bouts of anger. I stayed patient, though my flesh wanted desperately to lash out. I remember hour after hour, when everyone was going home, I was still doing my job. I turned my work towards the Lord. Nothing else could discourage me. I put myself to the test and submitted myself to the authority in charge of me. The authority had been established by God. He has gone on to say, "Those who rebel against the authorities is rebelling against Him and those who do so bring judgement on themselves" (Romans 13:2). I wanted to keep God's favor upon me. I learned that by doing this, I no longer conformed to the patterns of this world. I denied myself and became a living sacrifice, holy and pleasing to God, which became my spiritual act of worship (Romans 12:1-

2). A Nazarene's ultimate mission in life is to lay down their life for another person. There is no greater love than this. A Nazarene will think of others before himself. His heart shall always lead him to be courteous. He will be thoughtful in and out of season for all others, no matter race, color, creed, or religious affiliation. For example, he is last to serve himself and first to serve others. A Nazarene's word and handshake are his very promise (to his Savior Jesus Christ), the Supreme Commander and Chief. His yes is true, and his no is for keeps. There are no gray areas or compromises on his lips, for we are the tip of the sword.

E. Physical Fitness

"Fame is a vapor, popularity an accident, riches take wing, and only character endures" (Charles Swindoll).

"Experience is the hardest kind of teacher. It gives you the test first and the lesson afterward" (Unknown).

"You can tell a lot about a man by the way he treats those who can do nothing for him" (Unknown).

Discipline is a reflection of our appearance. To train one's self to obedience is discipline, moral, and physical. Training, training, and training is a Nazarene's way of life. We are always leading the way. Please be not confused. We recommend all personnel to have a medical evaluation prior to any physical activity. Physical fitness training not only helps you feel better, you look better. You are fit for work and activities. You should read health and fitness magazines to apprize yourself of the latest work outs and diets. I recommend no soft drinks during the week. Eight to ten cups of water a day. Then, reward yourself with one or two tea-flavored drinks on the weekend. Do not eat before you go to bed. Say goodbye to french fries! Say it. Goodbye french fries. Maybe once in a while? Fast food only once a week at the most. Dairy products need to be minimal. Learn to cook healthy and be responsible. Cook with only polyunsaturated oils. Watch your junk food. Portion control to the rescue. Small portions are the key. As for your workouts, be sure to exercise your heart with a cardio program. Remember, the person with the most wind wins the race or the fight.

Another good idea is to find a workout partner. Males with males and females with females. No exceptions; we have no other way. Of course, if you are married, that is a different story. Document your weight and take a picture of each other; one year later, take another. You will enjoy the results! Remember, it is about discipline. Do not be late to your training and set a schedule you both are able to meet. Do not leave your training buddy waiting for you. That is uncool. As a Nazarene, you are required to have physical fitness training tests every six months. Your sergeant in-charge will be responsible for providing the test and testing area. Military PT test charts have been available online at goarmy.com since late 2007 or early 2008. The categories are push-ups or pull-ups, sit-ups or leg raises, and the two-mile run or five-mile bike ride. You will be expected to pass at the minimum level. This is your act of discipline and your dedication to those who love you. Your scores will also help you to advance as a Nazarene soldier and a Saint. 2 Timothy 3:16-17 NIV

All Scripture is God-breathed and is useful for teaching, rebuking, correcting and training in righteousness, so that the servant of God may be thoroughly equipped for every good work. The US Marines have a very excellent saying, "Pain is weakness leaving the body!" I am crazy about that saying! No pain, no frame! Get fired up! Begin training ASAP; that is an order. (Do not forget your medical exam first?)

For physical training is of some value, but godliness (spiritual training) is of value in everything and in every way since it holds promise for the present life and for the life to come. 1 Timothy 4:8 NIV

F. Grade and Rank

"Quantum faith is the smallest molecule of energy called hope" (Adam P. Childress).

"Life is a grind stone. Whether it grinds you down or polishes you up depends upon what you are made of" (James S. Hewitt).

"The thing is to understand myself, to see what God really wishes me to do.to find the idea for which I can live and die" (Soren Kierkegaard).

Fellowships around the nation have developed many great programs to meet the needs of men and women of the church community. As we venture into our understanding of grade and rank, there is one idea I'd like to express. As you have read in the previous chapter, "Order and Balance" have a similar ring to it. God gives us our particular spiritual gifts and physical talents. As we mature in our walk with the Lord and begin to recognize our talents, we invariably discover our call-in ministry. Our church life takes on a new role in our day-to-day thinking. We have enlisted by faith into the most powerful military on the face of the universe. Some of us will be enlisted status and others will desire to become non-commissioned officers and commissioned officers. As most of you already know, enlisted and commissioned personnel have multiple levels. Being a young Christian soldier, you are not expected to be in authority over others until you mature. (Young means young in the faith, not age.) Character does not come with rank. You must endure through mission after mission to develop character and discipline. As in the military, he who leads the way makes the grade. You are recognized for your dedication to the tasks given. In the meantime, you are expected to read your soldiers' manual (bible) to grow in the knowledge of Christ's likeness, like all good soldiers do. We must hold the line together, shoulder to shoulder, soldier to soldier. You will also be expected to be a soldier under authority, as all other believers who have joined the ranks of a Christian soldier.

Let's try to make sense of what grade means for a Christian. Grade is defined as a step or stage in a course or process. A step or stage is very similar to a distance traveled in life. We have all experienced life's labor pains of adolescence and peer pressure. As we matured, we felt the responsibilities that came with being a young adult. Walking through life sets our course and leads us all into our decision-making process. Decisions are made based on moral aptitude and our belief system. This is influenced by our day-to-day decisions as we experience life. As Christians, we are influenced by our understanding of who Christ is in us. Some of us, due to toxic parents or radioactive religious thinking, have set a reverse course for our lives. Living in reverse requires U-turn after U-turn. No true standard of measurement. Only what feels right and good. What is in it for me attitude. We are now blown about by winds of shame and guilt. By reading this book I believe you want to live life above the city sanitation level and step up out of the garbage of this world. This is your time to make a U-turn and voluntarily enlist by faith in Christ's military service. Enlistment is simply joining the Christian faith and learning to be the best Christian soldier you can be. You may soldier your Christian faith by becoming a greeter at the front doors of your church, an usher, a parking lot attendant, a food server, a janitor, a child care provider, a youth assistant, a choir member, a provider of finances, a powerful prayer partner.

There are many other positions to be filled. If you feel a stronger desire to serve God's great military, seek the greater gifts. Maybe you're called to be a non-commissioned officer. As a non-commissioned officer, you have been entrusted as a leader of those ministries listed above. This is when you become missionary level. You could be called to become a commissioned officer. A commissioned officer has great responsibilities and much is required. You are a captain of the altar, senior armor bearer, leader of men or women groups, a teacher, a trainer, a preacher, a minister, a healer, a worship leader, and the list goes on. At this level, you are an evangelist in training until you become a captain or above. Then you are an evangelist. When you have reached this commitment level, you have been approved by those you have been serving. You have followed under authority and have been found worthy of the task. As a new believer, your first level of rank is a believer as an enlisted soldier. Also known as private enlisted number one. PVT 1 / E-1. The following breakdown will show the Nazarene rank structure:

Enlisted (Warriors of Light)
1.) PVT-E1—Believer

2.) PVT/E2—Seeker

3.) PVT/E3—Servant

4.) PVT/E4—Faithful

5.) Sergeant/E5—Missionary (mentors)

6.) SSgt/E6—Missionary Seeker (teachers)

7.) SFC/E7—Missionary Servant (recruiter)

8.) Master Sgt/E8—Missionary Faithful (Chaplin)

9.)First Sgt/E8—Missionary Shepard (Company Senior NCO)

10.) Sgt Major/E9—Missionary Eagle (Brigade NCO)

11.)Command/SgtMajor/E10—Missionary Sword (Divisional NCO)

Officer (Knights of Light)

1.) 2nd Lt/01—Alpha

2.) 1st Lt/02—Omega

3.) Captain/03—Evangelist

4.) Major/04—Evangelist Shepard

5.) Lt Col/05—Builder-the rock

6.) Col/06—Eagle (Chief builder)

7.) General/07—Spirit of God (lion's den)

8.) General/08—Word of God (lionhearted)

9.) General/09—Sword of the Word (lion keeper)

10.) General/10—Lion of Saints

11.) General/11—Shepard of the Nazarenes

This is exciting! Where do you fall in? Are you a staff

sergeant or a general? The way you can find out where you fall is to have three church members write you a letter of recommendation as to your character. Second, you write up your testimony and have three family members or close friends sign it to state to the best of their knowledge that your testimony is true. Third, you get a letter of ministry participation from any and all ministries you have led, assisted, or volunteered. Fourth, you will need certified copies of your qualifications (i.e., high school, military, college, correspondence courses, church courses, missions, and any other certificates to add to your qualifications). These certificates will help determine your rank. Fifth, you will be required to submit and pay for a background check. Some of us have made a mistake. A background check is for us to be informed of you and not to judge you. Decisions are based on case-by-case study.

For more information, go to extremenazarene.com. Who knows, maybe you will be the Nazarene commander of your community.

G. Uniform

"The world is God's epistle to mankind—His thoughts are flashing upon us from every direction" (Plato).

"Certain thoughts are prayer. There are moments when, whatever be the attitude of the body, the soul is on its knees" (Victor Hugo).

"The man who keeps busy helping the man below him won't have time to envy the man above him" (Henrietta Mears).

When you consider the word "uniform," several ideas come to mind. Uniform, as in military dress attire, is the first item we will address. How we dress often reflects how we feel about ourselves. The less we have on, the less we feel about ourselves when we are in the house of God. We do tend to dress on levels of confidence. As we expose our physical posture, we are sending a message. Some messages say, look at me. I am muscular, and I can take you out! Ladies dress to say, I have curves, boys, and there are no guard rails on this highway? Let us face it: it is out of control on both sides of the fence. I could give you countless rhetoric, but for the sake of losing heart, let us just say we have a problem! Male and female alike, we have lost our perspective on saintly morality and courtesy for our frailties. Modesty is the policy. Confrontation lacks appeal from the church pulpit. Truthfully, the pulpit should not have to address it. Our leaders have plenty of time to instill in the members the importance of modesty. Not a bunch of hall monitors and fashion cops; true family communication with gentleness and genuine love. Is it too much for us to inconvenience our own family members within the body of Christ to come to the Father's house dressed appropriately? We need to learn the meaning of modesty first.

A part of the military uniform is uniformity. The uniform is worn one way, according to military regulations. You cannot alter any portion of the uniform, or you will be doing push-ups until the sun goes down. This kind of confrontation is not easy, and I am not running for office either. I do not even want to be popular, for that matter. For a superior understanding of how to deal with those who need loving guidance as to what to wear at church, look up Pastor C.J. Mahaney online.

I felt like when it comes to our uniform of faith and the

Bible. I could answer most questions, especially on the spiritual uniform of faith. I was brought up in the church and taught well and life groups and home groups. I gained a lot which had gotten stored up in my heart.

I am bringing this up this, because it's tempting for me to say, "If you've been here or watched or listened to the reading and sermons on chapters 1 and 2, and you're tired of doctrinal or intellectual or head stuff that Paul has been dealing with, fear not! Chapters 3 and 4 have the application for understanding the need for a uniformed faith. Paul's going to tell us what to do, and how to get or keep your life on track." If we outline the book of Colossians, there is that shift, that difference in your march. Yet you and I must be careful to not completely divide these things, to say one part is for some and the other is completely for others.

No, what comes in chapters 3 and 4, moving into a clearer practical study, builds on the first two chapters. What we've heard and learned and believe about Christ is the reason why we do what we do. A person can implement all the moral actions they want into their lives without Christ, but why Paul teaches this, why God calls us to put on and keep on this new uniform of faith, because it flows out of what's gone before. This only reaches its desired uniformity, if the believer understands God's word, their inheritance, the training they must continue to do, and their struggle.

We are going to take up the commands of this passage for soldiering in three points. The first is what we find in verses 1 and 2, "…Set your hearts on things above, where Christ is seated at the right hand of God. Set your minds on things above, not on earthly things." As you've heard me saying through this book, we as Extreme Nazarenes, we recognize this command is for believers to train themselves, for those "who have been raised with Christ," who have "died, and your life is now hidden with Christ in God." There's no distinction among soldiers, though. This is just as much for the new or young Christians as it is for the older, more mature Christian. Wherever we feel we're at in life, combat or failures, our minds are to be set on things above and not on earthly things. We march to sound of Jesus Christ!

What does that mean, though? Is this talking about the affairs of the world? Are we being told, "Don't think about what's going on down here. Don't involve yourselves in the world or its problems. Ignore disasters and joys, forget about politics, media, and financial institutions. Just think about heaven"? That doesn't fit with the rest of Scripture, which calls us to love our neighbors as ourselves, to care and steward the creation, to weep with those who weep and rejoice with those who rejoice, to pray for those who are sick, to honor the king, to work and be generous with what we have. Thinking about heaven all day every day, to the point that we ignore anything else, is not Paul's message.

What's he saying, then? He is saying don't make it your primary objective. Heavon should always be our first instinct. The Bible does not say very much about heaven. But its central figure is clear: it is the place where the crucified Christ already reigns, our commander and king, where his people already have full rights of citizenship. To concentrate the mind on the character of Jesus Christ, on that unique blend of love and strength revealed in the Gospels, is to begin on earth to reflect the very life of heaven."

Rather than saying, "Forget about the affairs of this world, just think about heaven,". A person cannot pursue Christ by earthly means. You don't have him simply by focusing only on what you shall and shall not do on this earth. A life of good behavior does not earn or win grace for anyone.

To receive grace, redemption, salvation, we have to be looking to the Savior. Our hearts and minds must be fixed on what we heard in that middle section of Colossians 1—all that Jesus has done and how he is Savior and Lord overall. It's what we find in Philippians 2 verses 5 through 11, where Paul describes the journey of Christ—he, fully God and fully man, emptied himself, took human form, being obedient unto death, but with his resurrection and ascension, "God exalted him" to heaven, "to the highest place and gave him the name that is above every name, that at the name of Jesus every knee should bow, in heaven and on earth and under the earth, and every tongue confess that Jesus Christ is Lord, to the glory of God the Father."

If you have set your mind on things above or are wondering what that involves, it's setting your mind on Christ, which can only be done by faith, a uniform faith. When we're fixed on him, we are thinking of what he has done, of who he is, of what he's worth and deserves, of what he's able to do, we will be transformed by the Holy Spirit. We will be made new. We have died and been raise with Christ that is our identity and our uniform of faith. That happened, the One who is in heaven, regenerates who we are and what we should desire. Philippians 4:8, which is where we find, "whatever is true, noble, right, pure, Loving, admirable, excellent or praiseworthy." We all can change behavior, but being able to recognize and pursue those things which God wants is connected to who Christ. Soldiers who submit to his reign, worship, and praise for His glory. We must not swerve into ignorance towards the work and the exaltation of Jesus Christ and what that means for us. So, set your mind on the things above, not merely on things you can change day to day. My next point, the next command, builds on this. We don't get to choose the order of what comes first; it's given to us as a directive. Paul writes in verses 5, 8, and 9, "Put to death, therefore, whatever belongs to your earthly nature: sexual immorality, impurity, lust, evil desires, and greed, which is idolatry, you must rid yourselves of all such things as these: anger, rage, malice, slander, and filthy language from your lips. Do not lie to each other."

If you are focused on Christ, who died for you and for your sins, to bear the punishment of them, to redeem you from eternal death, to save your soul, why would you keep on living in sin? Soldiers don't keep on living in sin. It's because that's our nature when we come into this life; it's what we know even before we know it. Sin seems alluring, because the devil tells us it will satisfy, it will provide us with something we can't have otherwise. We so often accept the same lie that the serpent told Eve in the Garden, "You will not surely die." It's a little distraction to the absolute true of God.

Yet God's word, is the absolute truth and tells us, "Put to death whatever belongs to your earthly nature." We're not to flounder debating how to get out of it while continuing to do what we've been doing. Whatever is causing or encouraging us to sin, cease and desist! Invite help from your combat buddy. Use accountability as a strategy.

If we are focused on Christ, then it's time to get rid of the sin that is in our lives, especially the ones listed in our passage. All of these are things that it can be said, "Everyone does them." Yet as all our parents probably taught us, "Just because everyone else does something, doesn't mean you have to or should." We need to be careful. We need to put to death sexual sins, sins around greed and money, sins that exist during our relationships with people not to show pride, arrogance, or go overboard in proving that they are right. Why shouldn't we lie? Jesus himself spoke of the devil as having "no truth in him. When he lies, he speaks his native language, for he is a liar and the father of lies."

H. Weapons Qualification

"One of the marks of maturity is the ability to disagree without becoming disagreeable" (Charles R. Swindoll).

"My apparent lack of sophistication, doesn't make you a sudden genius" (Adam P. Childress).

"A godly man with discipline is unstoppable" (Delilah Drews).

There are three weapon-qualification badges you can receive when qualifying with your M-16A1 rifle. These badges range from a highly skilled expert, sharpshooter, and a marksman. These badges identify your skill level after qualifying with your weapon. As Nazarenes, we also find ourselves qualifying with our weapons (that the Holy Spirit provides us). "Wisdom is better than weapons of war" (Ecclesiastes 9:18). I realize, in order for any of us to survive one day on this planet or one minute on the battlefield, we must have wisdom from God's battle plans. In addition, we do not go anywhere without our armor and weapons of righteousness fully intact. "For though we live in the world, we do not wage war as the world does. The weapons we fight with are not the weapons of this world. On the contrary, we have divine power to demolish strongholds" (2 Co 10:3-4). We are soldiers who warrior against the devil's schemes. "Finally, be strong in the Lord and in His mighty power. Put on the full armor of God, so that you can take your stand against the devil's schemes. For our struggle is not against flesh and blood, but against rulers, and against authorities, against the powers of this dark world and against the spiritual forces of evil in the Heavenly realms" (Eph 6:10-12).

The Apostle Paul tells us to put on the armor and take up a stance. Sounds like spiritual telepathy or something out of Star Wars. May the force be with you. We say, may the Lord be with you. This means we have to battle our flesh because of the rulers, authorities, and powers of this dark world! They (the dark side) are going to do everything in their sphere of influence to trip us up. It is the dark side against the light side. We are soldiers of the light; we are the Nazarenes! Taking our stand means more than filling a spot on earth and digging your feet in. It means standing for what is right in the sight of our God. It means becoming a hero of the faith. The West was won only when the good guys started shooting back. As believers, we have to fight back with wisdom to stand firm. To say no to addictions, like drugs, porn, alcohol, fast food, T.V. roaming eyes, spending money, living beyond our means, and being in debt. The list is endless and the casualties are. mounting

We could spend hours going through what things fit into each of these categories, each of these sin labels. If you want to know more about sexual immorality and impurity, join us for the a morning Bible Study called back to the basics or B2B on the familyworshipcenterlasvegas.com There's plenty to unpack on a variety of levels. It's an oversimplification to say that when you see it, you know it's sin, but we can know what sin is by reading our Bibles our very manuals for living life. God has told us his ways—in detail like in the Ten Commandments and in these lists scattered across the New Testament—as in commanding us to love. We find out what God wants out of us by looking where he has spoken clear directives to us in our manuals.

Before we move on, I want to point out two significant sentences in addition to these commands. Verses 6 and 7, "Because of these, the wrath of God is coming. You used to walk in these ways, in the life you once lived." Brothers and sisters, we are not perfect, and we have not been. We're going to look in a moment at what we are called to put into practice in terms of what is good and godly versus what we're to be putting to death. But in our interactions with others, with those who are struggling in the faith or who we're hoping to see God bring to himself, when we see others in the mud of their sin, we should not think that we weren't ever in the same position. We shouldn't forget and think real Christians soldiers don't struggle or aren't burdened like so-and-so is struggling. That's not to say that every one of us has the same exact battles of sin and temptations; no, but we must remember we had and have sins that we still need to put to Christ's help to kill.

Setting our eyes on things above is first, putting earthly things to death is second. Why can't or why shouldn't a person think they can just fix their eyes on things above and ignore everything else, ignore the presence of sin and evil in their lives? The answer is what we heard in verse 6, "Because of [the sins of our earthly nature], the wrath of God is coming." Again, if we're grateful and trusting that we do and will continue to experience the riches of Christ's love, we shouldn't continue to do and see nothing wrong with the things that are bringing about his wrath.

I'm preaching to myself—I have my own sins that are part of this, that I need to rid myself of; I'm not claiming that I've got this dress-right dress with perfection. But believers cannot in good faith or good conscience ignore God and what he has told us is his will and what are his ways. He has revealed that for our good in our soldiers' manual, the Bible.

Put on the believer's uniform of faith and zero in your greatest weapon; hearts focused on truth. Much of this focuses on what I said earlier to the new believer. Verses 12 through 14, "Therefore, as God's chosen people, holy and dearly loved, clothe yourselves with compassion, kindness, humility, gentleness, and patience. Bear with each other and forgive whatever grievances you may have against one another. Forgive as the Lord forgives you. And over all these virtues put on love, which binds them all together in perfect unity." You're focused on Christ. Because of that and trusting the help of the Holy Spirit, you aim is putting things to death. What's taking their place, though? What's rising from the dirt or the ashes? What's springing to new life? Love in all these forms.

It's easy to say that these things should just be natural. Yet because of the presence of sin still trying to strangle us and hold a place in our lives, we must be intentional about leaving these things out. We are always adjusting our sights and changing elevation to hit the target. Stay focused or we will continue to be distracted piling up our lives with things.

What a great lie Satan has us believing. What is it? That we never have enough. We keep buying and storing what we already have! Now, we have valuables in storage for years and have paid for those items five times over! The rent to store what we do not need is ridiculous and ludicrous. Do you know where all the extra money we spend is supposed to go? How about the money we are spending to store what we hardly ever use?

Yes, you are right—the church and those in need. Not into the pastor's pocket. However, your pastors should be well paid or shame on your church. The Lord rebuke you if not. Ouch, so do not elect me! I am not running for office or a popularity contest. Will I ever stop saying that? All believers were of one heart and mind. No one claimed that any of his possessions were his own. They shared everything they had. With great power, the apostles continued to testify to the resurrection of the Lord Jesus Christ, and much grace was upon them all. There were no needy persons around them (Acts4:32-34). We have needy people in every city and state across America. More around the world who have nothing. We are embezzling God's money for our own pleasures. We continue to store it away like a hidden talent. "But the man who had received one talent went off, dug a hole in the ground and hid his master's money" (Mt 25:18).

Daddy was not happy when he came back. "Then the man who had received one talent came. Master, he said, I knew that you are a hard man, harvesting where you have not sown and gathering where you have not gathered seed. So, I was afraid and went out and hid your talent in the ground. See, here is what belongs to you" (Mt 25:24-25). We could say the same and just change a few words. Here Daddy, the money you gave me is in the storage shed I had rented. Are we afraid to invest it into the Kingdom? I say as long as there are people in need, let us give them what we are not using. Our money used to store our goodies is like throwing it into the wind needlessly. Let us all become responsible. We should give it to the church to delegate and distribute. They will be held highly accountable. This is truly a stronghold we can break. We have the weapon of wisdom to destroy the enemy. We must break the habitual rhetoric and worldly perspective to focus on our weapons of righteousness. Therefore, put on the full armor of God, so when the day of evil comes, you may stand your ground, and after you have done everything to stand just stand (Eph 6:13). When does the day of evil come? For you, it may be today. For someone else, it may be tomorrow. And for others, it may be every minute. In the military, you are told to never take off your cavalier (helmet). When you least expect it, you could get hit. You are told never to fall asleep on duty, or you may be found by another lying on the ground. Lying without your weapon in your hands. You are taught readiness as a necessity for alertness. You are to never be caught off guard. So, stand your ground and when all hell breaks loose, just stand because God said so. It is the moment of truth. Obedience and willingness to follow Christ to the cross no matter what fight, battle, or war we are in! No matter the number of casualties or if you are wounded. Stand! Stand! Stand! For the name of Christ, stand your ground!

I. Wisdom and Discipline

"Christians become preoccupied with their failures; from then on, the battle is won" (C.S. Lewis).

"God honors no drafts where there are no deposits" (The Defender).

"Integrity is to be practiced in private and modeled in public." (Adam P. Childress).

"For attaining wisdom and discipline; for understanding

words of insight; for acquiring a discipline and prudent life, doing what is right and just and fair; for giving prudence to the simple, knowledge and discretion to the young-let the wise listen and add to their learning, and let the discerning get guidance" (Proverbs 1:2-5). If a Nazarene would be awarded a badge of wisdom and discipline, the words typed on the certificate would reflect Proverbs 1:2-5. This would be the "Christ-like" certificate of accomplishment. Not a lifetime achievement award but a lifestyle achievement award. After reading Proverbs 1:2-5, can you think of anyone you have known since you have been a Christian that would be qualified for such an award or certificate? Who, in your opinion, has accomplished this example? Is it you? Is it your best friend or mentor?

Wisdom and discipline go hand in hand. Discipline means to be trained to act in accordance with rules. Wisdom means the quality or state of being wise: knowledge of what is true or right coupled with good judgment. Sounds like possessing good discernment and discretion. This leads us to a standard of living and decision-making process. We all live by a standard and make all our decisions based on our so-called truths and experiences. I tell you the truth, pack up all of those mental books and past experiences. Throw them into the nearest trash can. There is a new standard you live by and are now judged under. How will we measure up under the new standard?

Standard is defined as morals, ethics, and habits based on an established authority, custom, or individual as acceptable. When we first heard the good news of Christ, we accepted it by faith, the price our Savior has paid for our sins, our debt, or trust. We put Christ in charge of our trust. Trust is defined as confidence in the certainty of future payment (Christ's blood shed for us). His blood covers all who believe and join in the ranks of the saints. Changing our old nature and becoming a new nature is a conflict with Satan's interest in us. We may be born into sin. We are now born again into grace by faith; amazing grace!!!

Hoo-Raw!!! Pick them up and put them down. Forty inches all around! Sound off!!!

J. Chow Time

"What we need are critical lovers of America-patriots who express their faith in their country by working to improve it" (Hubert H. Humphrey).

"A man's true wealth is the good he does in this world" (Beneixline).

"The high destiny of the individual is to serve rather than to rule" (Albert Einstein).

Jesus answered, "It is written: Man does not live by bread alone, but on every word that comes from the mouth of God" (Matthew 4:4). As we carefully examine the words Christ spoke, we can take comfort in knowing the only answer we give to our enemy is the sword of the Spirit, the word of God. Unlike Adam, who stood by while the tempter came to them in the garden and spoke to his bride. Adam could have said, "We are not to eat from the tree that is in the middle of the garden" (Genesis 3:3). However, Eve ate of it! Adam had all the authority necessary to tell the tempter where he could go. Christ submitted himself to God as Eve should have submitted herself to Adam. I believe the devil played Eve to see if Adam would step in or up. The devil's plan worked. God said to Adam (Gen 3:17), "Because you listened to your wife and ate from the tree about which I commanded you: You must not eat of it." The devil tricked Eve, and Adam just stood there and listened.

Our only defense is the Sword of the Spirit. We must speak up! Especially if we are to do battle with the tempter. Christ had all the divine power of heaven in a blink of an eye. All the angels at His command and Father God as his mighty fortress. Jesus accomplished his mission without using any majestic supernatural power. He used his sword, the supernatural power in action. "For the word of God is living and active. Sharper than any double-edged sword, it penetrates even to dividing soul and spirit, joints and marrow; it judges the thoughts and attitudes of the heart" (Hebrews 4:12). There is a lot to take in, so let us break it down like a recipe since we are speaking about our daily bread. For bread is essential to the body as the word of God is to the soul. First, the word of God is living and active. What does that mean? Living means the word of God will accomplish its mission. For example, Christ died and rose again as the word said he would (Luke 24:46). Active means it influences everything ever created. It is the very evidence that nothing in creation is hidden from God's sight (Heb 4:12). Sharper than any double-edged sword means divine judgment. The ultimate authority in existence. It penetrates even to dividing soul and spirit, joints and marrow; it judges the thoughts and attitudes of the heart. In my opinion, it is the standard of measurement used to weigh our deeds in our final moment (Heb 10:30). I am not speaking of the great white throne. It is the Bema Seat of Judgement. This is for you and I, who are believers in Christ. There we will be judged for the decisions we made while living our lives sworn to oath by our confession of faith in Christ Jesus. He is our Holy Supreme Commander and Chief. High-speed Nazarene!!! Chow time! Get in line! Stand at parade rest.

So, brothers and sisters, get dressed with a uniform of compassion. As I've seen many of you do and encourage you to continue, be present with others, be near to them when they suffer in hard times. Clothe yourselves with kindness. When someone is in need, be willing to help them out. Be willing to feed their souls. We aren't to care just about ourselves and people who fit into our likeness, our camp, our way of thinking, but we're to be kind to all. Put on humility. Don't brag about yourself, don't always count yourself better than other people; encourage and urge others to growth, praise them when they do well, when you see someone growing, even if they haven't reached where you hope and want them to be, lift them up. Show them the manna from Heaven is strengthening their faith! Put on is patience—take your time, do not rush. When interacting with others, listen and wait, serve them and fed them with a calmness. Even when we really want to sprint ahead, we know what we're capable of, journey beside someone at the pace they need. All these virtues are principles from above—this is the uniform that believers should put on to imitate and glorify Christ while at the chow line!

The Christian life can be filled with these fruits, only when we know our identity is in Christ. To be "God's chosen people," chosen by him!" To be his "holy and dearly loved," is also to have his peace ruling in our hearts, thankfulness in our lives because of him, his word dwelling in us as we share it. All this because of the preparation and continuing work that God is up to. It all requires love. As we address sin in our own lives and help others, may genuine love rooted in Christ always be our genuine desire. May that love guide us, not only to get rid of sin, but to follow-through in putting on and living into the uniform faith in Christ has given us, all while fixing our eyes on him and sharing the fruit of the Spirit!

K. Preventative Maintenance Checks and Services

"True heroism is remarkably sober, very undramatic. It is not the urge to surpass all others at whatever cost, but the urge to serve others at whatever the cost" (Arthur Ashe).

"I must study politics and war that my sons may have liberty to study mathematics and philosophy" (John Adams, 2nd President of the USA).

"Cherish your visions and dreams as they are the children of your soul; the blue prints of your ultimate achievements" (Napoleon Hill).

In short, we'll say PMCS. I always enjoyed the opportunity to fill out the PMCS paper and turn it in to the motor sergeant or my section chief.... NOT! At the time, it seemed like this was a huge joke or just another military way to hurry and wait. Now, well I am very grateful I paid close attention to the preventative maintenance paperwork. Upon receiving orders from Desert Shield, each section of the company had to produce twelve months of completed PMCS documentation for each vehicle assigned to that section. In addition, everything on back order was quickly delivered. Finally, during our first ground-breaking maneuvers, my Duce-in-a-half (2 ½ ton cargo truck) did not break down due to the upkeep and regular services my truck received. I cannot express the severity of keeping good documentation and continued preventative measures as a determined discipline in your life. For example, when I married my wife at the tender age of twenty years old. Yes, twenty years old and proud of it! She was more advanced in the competency of automobile mechanics than I was by far. I needed her help to locate the dipstick and found out (I was) the dipstick. I knew nothing better than where the gas cap was located and how to fill it. I was a serious rookie and mechanics had not been my strong suit. Even my wife's mother knew more than me.

I have learned from the best in the military. Years later, I have learned to keep up with our vehicles and plan all our preventative checks and services on paper. Keeping track of your last oil change, pressure in your tires, fluid levels, and brake pads' thickness is not easy when it has not been tracked. Do not forget all the warranties and services purchased in addition to the day you bought the vehicle. Maintenance also encompasses your home, your family, your wife or husband. Your home needs a great amount of your attention. The grass, irrigation, tree trimming, security, lights, roof leaks, painting, woodworking, fence repair, brick repair, plumbing repairs, sheet rock, electrical, doors, and windows. We must keep excellent records of the responsibilities God has entrusted to us. We are to be good stewards and consider all we own to be a PMCS. Our hearts need daily PMCS as we grow in Christ. Tracking our lives through the word of God is sure to keep us from breaking down. Nothing like shipwrecked faith! Dashed against the rocks of life. Family member overboard! "Hold onto to faith and good conscience, some have rejected these and so have ship wrecked their faith" (1 Timothy 1:19).

Our faith is located so deep in our hearts and wonderfully expressed through our daily actions. It is the very time of our expressions of faith that keeps us from blowing a flat tire along the freeway of life. Unfortunately, some of us forget to check the "air" of Christ's word" or "error" of our decisions. We end up blowing out a tire while speeding down the freeway of life. Now, we may be part-time PMCS personnel, and a wreck may not happen. Maybe, we do not maintain our faith, but on Sunday's alone. Leaving six days a week living reckless and unfaithful resulting in an unexpected head-on collision We must stay in God's word and constantly maintain preventative checks and services of our soul condition. You get the picture. Our growth depends on a new learning curve, with faith as its guardrails. Let us be excellent stewards of all we have and all that we can be in Christ Jesus. You are the most important being Christ died for. That is excellent life insurance only Jesus can cover. Keep your heart in balance, or you could be a liability.

L. The Nazarene dual Pledge of Allegiance

"A thoughtful mind, when it sees the nation's flag, sees not the flag only, but the nation itself" (Henry Ward Beecher).

"God is able to make all grace abound toward you" (2 Corinthian 9:8).

"As the earth can produce nothing unless it is fertilized by the sun, so can we do nothing without the grace of God" (Vianney).

I pledge allegiance to the flag of the United States of America and to the Republic for which it stands, one nation under God, indivisible, with liberty and justice for all. I Pledge allegiance to the Christian flag and to the Savior for whose Kingdom it stands: one brotherhood, uniting all mankind in service and love. The pledge of allegiance is the person's solemn oath of fidelity, promise, or agreement. This is your deepest promise of heart and soul, coming from everything you understand to be true and worthy of your death. There is no greater love than that of a man who would lay down his life for another. We have been privileged to experience this love due to our combat brothers and sisters who faced death for us. We shall gladly pledge our allegiance with a radical commitment to God, country, family and faith. We must wear our commitment with a uniformed faith. We should all look the same to those who know Christ and to those who do not. This is the optimum result of our basic training, our uniformed faith in Christ. How can we march alike if all of us Christians are marching in different directions, resulting in confusion and disbelief? We have so many arguments about our opinions and viewpoints. The devil is falling out of his fiery chair, laughing at our foolishness. His demons are drunk off our puffed-up wisdom and knowledge. Our basic training brings us a simple, disciplined, uniformed faith in Christ.

Apostle Paul had written to Timothy concerning the same point I was making. "As I urged you when I was in Macedonia, stay there in Ephesus so that you may command certain men not to teach false doctrines any longer nor to devote themselves to myths and endless genealogies. This promotes controversies rather than God's work—which is by faith. The goal of this command is love, which comes from a pure heart, a good conscience and sincere faith. Some have wandered away from these and turned to meaningless talk. They want to be teachers of the law, but they do not know what they are talking about or what they so confidently affirm" (1 Timothy 1:3- 7).

Wow! That does spell it straight out. We must have a

uniform faith in order to know the A-B- C's of our faith. A: You admit you are a sinner. B: You believe Jesus died for your sins (all of them and the ones to come). C: You confess with your heart, soul, and mouth that Jesus is your Lord God and Savior, that he has risen and is seated at the right hand of God! Now, the rest is walking in love, an expression of a pure heart, a good conscience with sincere faith. This is a command and not an option. It is extremely important to read God's word every day until you have come to a clear understanding of His will for your life."No longer will a man teach his neighbor, or a man his brother, saying, know the Lord, because they will all know me, from the least to the greatest" (Hebrews 8:11). "It is God's will for you that you be sanctified, that you should avoid sexual immorality, that each of you should learn to control his own body in a way that is holy and honorable, not in passionate lust like the heathen, who do not know God; and in this matter no one should wrong his brother or take advantage of him" (1 Thessalonians 4:3-6).

This is truly a posture of Christian soldiery. Our attitude is the altitude of our heart. As our daily walk is perfected, we are in basic training. Be sure not to lose your unique personality and sense of humor. God first loved you just as you were. We posture a heart of thankfulness. Time begins to foster in us patience for our fellow Christians and soldiers. Many of us have grown up without our fathers or mothers (even brothers and sisters). Some of us have even experienced the foster home life. I, too, had lived in foster care. Care—you mean foster survival care! The system was designed to foster a family home life. Some homes, I imagine were well-meaning. As brothers and sisters, we foster the love of Christ in us. Life is not a matter of chance but a matter of choice. We choose life. This means to model forgiveness which is the key to Christian maturity. No maturity, no growth. No growth, no freedom, and we deny the essence of Christ power in us. Now we see, we really do not know Him at all; we only know about Him. You received God's love, but rejecting His power means your hope is empty. You walk in contempt of God's righteous courts of mercy. Receive His power today, right now. Beloved, He loves you so. Kneel with me right where you are and receive these words meant for you and me. "Blessed is the man who perseveres under trial, because when he has stood the test, he will receive the crown of life that God has promised to those who love Him" (1 James 1:12).

I pray God's blessings over you. May you be filled to overflowing. May hope be your strength. If this message was for you, will you email me? I would like to personally say, "Welcome home, soldier, welcome home."

M. Dual Citizenship

"God opposes the proud but gives grace to the humble" (James 4:6).

"I have a dream that one day this nation will rise up and live out the true meaning of its creed: WE HOLD THESE TRUTHS TO BE SELF-EVIDENT, THAT ALL MEN ARE CREATED EQUAL" (Martin Luther King Jr.).

"I can make a lord, but only the Almighty can make a gentleman" (King James I).

As Nazarene, we are privileged to live both in the heavenly world and the earthly world. Our names take up residence in two addresses. The home we will occupy when we enter the sweet graces of our Father's house and the new heaven. This is similar to our bodies as we exist physically and spiritually. In addition, we live by the laws of this world and the laws of our hearts provided by the Spirit of the living God. As a soldier of Jesus Christ (a Nazarene soldier), we do not get involved in civilian affairs (worldly living and social politics). We want to please our commanding officer (2 Tim 2:3).

Apostle Paul spoke to Timothy about fighting the good fight, holding on to faith and a good conscience. He continued by saying some have rejected these and so have shipwrecked their faith (1 Tim 1:18-19). Civilian affairs, for example, would be knowing who is who in Hollywood, watching the news night and day (I am not saying trash can all news and television). We cannot be stuck on bogus political mudslinging and/or whatever the latest world scandal may be. These things have no place in the life of a Nazarene soldier. Needless information to occupy what little time we have. This non-information is exhausting and time-consuming. The enemy wants to distract us in any way, shape, or form. Pornography, poverty, and power are the major time distractions. Pornography allows the viewer to become one with the internet. Thus, destroying the family and cutting short its mortality. The mortality of the family to have any real chance of survival is in the hands of men. Our forefathers shaped this country, and our biological fathers are murdering it second by second. Prisons are filled with bio-fathers. Their decisions have left our homes fatherless. Homes are left to faithless children with no supervision and zero authority. Porno teaches our bio-son how to treat our daughters while they are on dates. Porno teaches our bio-daughters how to misbehave around our sons. Single mothers are too busy working and paying the bills to be fathers too! Although, some mothers do a dam good job of it! We love you, single parents. Where is the money to pay the bills? Poverty keeps us under pressure to just survive. We continue to live off our credit cards and live a lie. Deeper and deeper, we fall behind. We strive to get ahead. When we get ahead, finally, power and money have a way of becoming the root of all evil. We start loving money.

Money means the power to make choices, change policies, and enforce the law of personal opinion anywhere. Some make it their absolute ambition in life. They strive to be rich and powerful until the day they die. You can take nothing with you when you die. If handled correctly, money can be the leverage soldiers need to gain decision-making power in their lives, not the love of money. We must be extremely mature and wise and walk in serious understanding to not become corrupted by the power of money. Satan's hand grenade, a fist full of cash. With the other hand filled with worldly positions and corporate titles. Our tithe is a revelation of our maturity in Christ, and the amount of income we produce is the depth of trust our Savior has extended to us for a season. As we grow in faith, we step out in faith and we begin to make sound decisions. We begin backing them up with commitment and action towards accomplishing the promise we made. For every commitment we accomplish, we are pressed forward toward the goal of promotion through wisdom and maturity. Pick'em up and putt'em down! March on, march onward, Christian soldier! March as to war!!!

Chapter 2: Combat Readiness

A. Soldier of Amor

"Perhaps there is no happiness in life so perfect as the martyr's" (O. Hennery).

"Being all fashioned of the self-same dust, let us be merciful aswell as just" (Henry Long fellow).

"It is only one step from toleration to forgiveness" (Sir Arthur Wing Pinero).

When you consider the thought of armor, do you think of heavy metal? I cannot stop thinking of the days of the 10th through the 16th centuries. Those suits consisted of eighteen components. How did they scratch that itch? Do not look at me. Hee, hee, smiley face. Well, thank God our armor weighs as much as the spoken word; a mire vapor. "Therefore, put on the full armor of God, so that when the day of evil comes, you may be able to stand your ground" (Ephesians 6:13). Best part of this verse is, speak the words and your armor is on. Weightless and powerful.

As you probably know, when Apostle Paul wrote this passage, he was in chains in a Roman prison. As we can see clearly, the depiction is a soldier in his armor. Exactly what we are to practice putting on daily. I have used this scripture time and time again in this book. Every time you read it, you put it on by faith. This is our act of faith. To repeat scripture over and over. In modern combat, you are happy to carry as much ammo and protective gear as you possibly can. See, cover and conceal will keep you alive a lot longer. Ammunition and equipment extinguish the enemy. While in combat, you do not take off anything because it maybe the very item that saves your life.

Your spiritual armor does the same thing. The enemy gets in your face. Demons enjoy beating you on your head, neck, back, and feet, sticking and jabbing all over, looking for weaknesses in your armor. So, the question is, are you wearing it? Have you sat it on a chair? How rusty is it? Is it on a shelf collecting dust? Does it have holes, cracks, and tears now? Maybe you have been battling without your armor and received multiple wounds? Friend, you are not defeated or alone. You will heal with the mercy of Christ. Trust and forgive those who have wounded you. Healing is only proceeded by true forgiveness, letting go and trusting God. If you are a wounded soldier, put your armor back on right now and confess to the Lord your failure. Trust in the Lord your God. "For our struggle is not against flesh and blood, but against the rulers, against the authorities, against the powers of this dark world and the spiritual forces of evil in the heavenly realms" (Ephesians 6:12).

The metaphor of full armor suggests more than just a suit of armor. The helmet of salvation means to set your mind on things above (Col 3:2-3). Now, your helmet of salvation can protect your head from harm. You need to wear it, in other words. The breastplate of righteousness protects your heart so that nothing can penetrate your heart and fool your spirit. "He put His spirit in our hearts as a deposit, guaranteeing what is to come" (2 Corinthians 1:22). We can get so distracted by the foolish antics of the enemy's scams. The shield of faith is used to block the fiery arrows of the evil one (As it says in Eph 6:16). The sword of the spirit is used to fight the spiritual battle, to tear down strongholds and to come against the unseen ambushes. This sword is a double-edged sword, and it is the very word of God. You need to practice with your sword. Train yourself in the discipline of spiritual tactics. When the Apostle Paul was chained in Rome, his writing bore his personal signature, as did all the other apostles. The Apostle Paul's was an open bible laid over the gladius sword of Rome. This became known as, "Spiritus Gladius" in Latin. In English, it means "Sword of the Spirit!" The Gladius sword was the sword that conquered the world as the Romans knew it to be. Now, the Sword of the Spirit will be the sword that conquered the world as we now know it to be. "Spiritus Gladius" are words which inspire the heart! Say these words often, and you will surely stir yourself up for spiritual warfare. We are warriors and knights of Godslight! The belt of truth is not for holding up your righteous trousers!

The belt of truth is to keep you standing secure in your hope in who Christ is in this life (Ephesians 6:14). Living the truth is proof of character. Character never forces its way in brute strength but reveals the enemy in the deception of his stance. We must prepare for vigorous action, for righteousness in truth. It is our belt fitted for battle. "Righteousness will be his belt and faithfulness the sash around his waist" (Isaiah 11:5).

B. Soldier of Velvet

"Each life has the ability to touch yet more lives. And so, person by person, generation by generation, a world and a future are shaped" (Thomas Kinkade).

"Let music swell the breeze, and ring from all the trees, sweet freedom ring" (Samuel F. Smith).

"I like the dreams of the future better than the history of the past" (U.S. President Thomas Jefferson).

The definition of velvet means smooth and/or soft. Sometimes, smooth is the last thing I am. Soft seems contradictory to my masculine character. What do you mean by a man of velvet? Let us look at it in terms of who we are to our families. A soldier who cares and gives his family presence, not presents. Kids spell love T-I-M-E. We all know from experience whatever our parents did for us or lack of, reflects on how we perceive ourselves in terms of value. Our choice to change history can begin with how we choose to spend our time. Time dictates our values. Who pays the price when we spend time on the market of life? When we spend our time filled with exterior ambition (other than our families and kingdom activities, we can consider it the black market). This is when we find ourselves gambling with our families as valued commodities. We wager a hefty value when we step into the black market. Your family becomes the commodity of timeshare. To gamble our family on the black market of time is a travesty and highly criminal!

No husband, wife, or child should be wagered due to our lack of time management and personal agendas. We must be men and women who are considerate and listen to other's needs and feelings. The word compassionate comes to mind. That is a part of soft as velvet I would like to identify with. It is ridiculous to have all the time in the world to listen to the needs and feelings of those you are mentoring. When you get home finally, you have absolutely nothing left for your family. How can we keep ripping them off? My wife said something I will never forget. She said, "Look, I do not want your leftovers. I need your first course." I decided this was a good day to increase my value for her and be a strategic time manager. I needed to start a new school of thought and learn to communicate; share everything with her. She needs to know I value her and mutually respect her time. I will share this point with you. My wife is a lady who receives her value by what she sees me communicate to her: My thoughts, my time, my touch, my attention, and my response all speak velvet value. These qualities have everything to do with time, care, and love for one another. This conduct is quite becoming of a soldier and a believer. Really, it is simple: it is being courteous to our eternal love for one another. Family, make the most of every opportunity, for the time is short (Col 4-5). Let us stop gambling with our future and lay hold of some genuine fun with our loved ones.

C. Soldier of Steel

"Let us by all wise and constitutional measures promote intelligence among the people as the best means of preserving our liberties" (James Monroe 5th U.S. President).

"Until a man is nothing; God can make nothing out of him"(Martin Luther).

"You will be as small as your controlling desire, as great as your dominant aspiration" (James Allen).

Have you ever heard someone say, "metal has memory?" When metal is bent, it will flex back. A soldier of steel is a person who can bend and flex under pressure and with the ability to bounce back! Such a person is tempered. Tempered steel has been heated and cooled, forged to perfection. When steel has been heated to a certain temperature, the impurities separate from the metal, which is called metallurgy. I believe God allows the heat in our lives to reach the point of separation in order to purify us for his sake. Soldier, when in a rage, create a fire of enormous intensity of wrath. Men experience anger on a level not experienced by most ladies, in my opinion. A father should never use his power of rage in his home to govern. The only time such rage should ever be expressed in any manner is to protect his family. For example, if someone were coming through the front door uninvited with bad intentions. Abuse of this rage has been recorded throughout the world. Has anyone taught our men how to walk away and cool off? Such a simple decision.

The police reports documenting spouse abuse are staggering and shameful. Child abuse is an epidemic. Men and women are filling the jail cells of America. Children are left hopeless, broken, and unprotected. The enemy enjoys this period of time in the child's life. Why? He becomes the voice in their heads and accuser of the broken home. Satan begins to speak a new language that only they can understand. This vernacular speaks to the very weakest nature of that little person. It is at this time in the child's life when they develop their personality. Here is where the devil posts a demon to feed the young soul the lies of ancient serpent venom. Poisoning the child with accusations such as, see, no one loves you. You're so stupid. You are always going to be worthless. You will never measure up. You are a loser, just give it up. Do not even try because you will just give in again. Everyone else gets away with it, so just drink it, smoke it, and swallow it too. Many other words can be used here in place of the ones I have written. You can fill in the blanks, unfortunately. I still battle with the word venom my parents used. When the words arise in my soul like oozing blisters, I apply forgiveness like baby lotion. I speak words of healing over my heart and get rid of those salt feelings like an old rash.

Words express communication, and communication (sadly) becomes your native language. Please go to your soldier's manual and turn to (2 chron 32). Here, the king of Assyria came to invade Judah. King Hezekiah fortified the walls and even the inner cities. He blocked off the water from the springs. Blocking off the water was a great idea. Who is going to want to live somewhere desolate? Hezekiah then patched the walls and had them build strong towers to watch over the land. In addition, they built a large number of shields and weapons. He appointed officers over the people and assembled them, saying, "Be strong and courageous, do not be afraid or discouraged, because of the king of Assyria and the vast army with him, for there is a greater power with us than with them. With his there is only the arm of flesh, but with us is the Lord our God to help us fight our battles" (2 Chronicles 32:7- 8). They are flesh and we have the Lord your God to help fight our battle. They were still a bit fearful. With their eyes on the Lord, they gained courage, but the odds were still surmounting. The battles started in nearby cities, and the enemy sent a battle-gram to Hezekiah and the people in the city. First strategy, break down their confidence and appeal to their fear. Second, he reminded them of past defeats at the hands of his father. Third, he provokes their faith to question the power and existence of their God. Fourth, they wrote letters of intimidation, affecting them on a long-term basis and appealing to their logic to cancel out their hope. Fifth and final point, they spoke to the watchmen on the towers in their native language. They were able to speak fear straight into their hearts to make them come down from their secure position to slaughter them.

Your new language is superior to your native language. Today, you speak with courage, joy, peace, forgiveness, power, and authority to demolish the stronghold in Jesus' name! If someone speaks to you in your native language, answer them only in your new language. This will be like dropping hot coals on their heads. Speaking love and kindness to your enemy makes them want to self-combust. Do not back down from the enemy. Stand your ground in full armor and speak these words. "Devil, Jesus rebuke you!" You have cut the throat of your enemy. He must flee with his fatal wound. You must be sincere in your kindness in all things. The Devil knows your old personality. He would love to see you sin in your anger. Always be genuine and transparent. It is our time to show military bearing in action. Character will say all that is needed to be said. We will keep the Devil guessing. He cannot speak your new language; it is foreign to him. This will keep him on the run. He does not understand what you are saying and no longer knows you. He cannot accuse you. He can only remind you in your native language. The voice you choose to listen to determines the outcome of the battle. You demonstrate a uniform faith in Jesus Christ. He is the Mightiest military commander to ever step foot on His creation!

D. Tour of Duty

"A wise man has great power, a man of knowledge increasesin strength; for waging war you need guidance, and for victory you need many adviser" (Prov 24:5-6).

"Success is when I add value to myself. Significance is when Iadd value to others" (John C. Maxwell).

"A thoughtful mind, when it sees a nations flag, sees not theflag only, but the nation itself" (Henry Ward Beecher).

Our time is now! We must make the most of every opportunity, for the time is short (Col 3). Time is not on our side but on our backs. Some carry time as if they have no end. Wisdom says, "But the end of all things is at hand, therefore be serious and watchful in your prayers" (1 Pet 4:7). Our nation is suffering the worst statistics recorded in our generation to date. It is embarrassing and incomprehensible. It is discouraging, but we must be watchful, as Peter warned. Time has run out for us to spend every moment changing policies and making laws to fit our agenda. "Train a child in the way he shall go, and when he is old, he will not turn from it" (Proverbs 22:6). Train a soldier in his duty to Christ, and when the battle is at hand, he will stand never to depart. In our men's group, we have a new saying, it is called, "Not on my watch!" A very powerful statement. Your tour of duty will have its challenges, but what happens on our watch will make all the difference. What you allow on your watch can determine the outcome of your destiny and those you have been entrusted with. As fathers, mothers, brothers, sisters' husbands, wives, and Christian soldiers, we have a serious mission. As for me and my house, we will serve the Lord! (Josh 24:15) In our individual churches, the need for male participation is greatly absent. As a Nazarene, it is our duty to fill in the needs of the local church. We are to be trained by those in charge. In return, train others to fill our position as they show themselves faithful. Your church may already have training in place. I encourage you to begin your military career praying how you can best fill a ministry position, serving someone first. Pray only once about it and march right into action. You do not need to hear from God to get involved. Your prayer is to guide you to the right people. Stop wasting God's time and get busy with kingdom business. Our ability to influence the next two generations of young men and women is more than probable; it is destiny!

As a Christian, we have been silent too long. We have lost our right to lead without question. We must earn our leadership back! God opened the doorway of salvation to the Gentiles because the Israelites were unfaithful, forgetful, and downright sinful. God did this to stir them up. To provoke them too jealously! To motivate them into action! They loved the law and not God's grace. They forgot their first love. We are just like the men and women of yesterday. We have faith amnesia today. It is time to reverse history for our tomorrow. Nazarene are all about tomorrow. I believe God has opened the door to the women of our churches to provoke men into action. Some men are waking up to this. Some men are so used to their wives making all the decisions at home. They would rather follow instead of being the leader of their homes. It is your duty to lead your home men. It is equally important for the wife to co-lead. She carries the authority of her husband in his absence. Husbands carry the burden of judgement. God will hold him strictly accountable. This is the time and place for your tour of duty to become your permanent party. Ask yourself what is your weakness as a husband? Write it down! Listen, soldier, I said write it down! You need to lead your family with Godly principles. It is time to participate in the greatest revolution of our time. The full recovery of the family unit. We are the sons and daughters of liberty. Constituting principles of a Nazarene soldier are as follows:

Constituting Principals of a Nazarene Soldier

1) **The soldier's duty is to serve others:** Let a man so consider us, as servants of Christ and stewards of the mysteries of God. Now it is *required* that those who have been given a trust *must prove faithful* (1 Corinthians 4:1-2). We are therefore *Christ's ambassadors,* as though God were making his appeal through us. So, we fix our eyes not on *what is seen,* but what is unseen. For what is seen is *temporary*, but what is unseen is *eternal* (2 Corinthians 4:18).

2) **Obedience to duty with selfless obligation**: Duty to one's *family*, duty to one's *church*, duty to one's *country* and one's duty to *tell the truth* as dictates in the inner most heart of hearts. This is *love,* that we walk in obedience to his *commands*. As you have heard from the beginning, His *command* is that you *walk in love* (2 John 6).

3) **Excellence of moral character:** Honorable virtuous *conduct.* Whatever happens,   conduct yourselves in a manner *worthy* of the *gospel of Christ* (Philippians 1:27).

Standard bearer in all things; be *self-controlled* and *alert.* Your enemy, the Devil, prowls around like a lion, looking for someone to *devour.* Resist him, *standing firm* in the faith [duty], because you know your fellow soldiers *throughout* the world are undergoing the same kind of *suffering* (1 Peter 5:8-9).

4) **Loftiness of mind and spirit:** His grace is *sufficient* for you, for *my power* is made perfect in *weakness.* Therefore, I will boast all the more gladly about my weakness, so that *Christ's power* may rest on me. That is why, for Christ's sake, I delight in weaknesses, insults, hardships, persecutions, and in difficulties. *For when I am weak, then I am strong* (2 Corinthians 12:9-10).

5) **In pursuit of knowledge, wisdom and understanding:** Fear of the *Lord* is the beginning of *knowledge* (Proverbs 1:7). The Lord gives *wisdom* and from His mouth comes *knowledge* and *understanding.* (Proverbs 2:6) *Train yourself to be godly* (1 Timothy 4:7). A student is not above his teacher, but everyone who is fully trained will *be like* his teacher (Luke 6:40). *Follow* my example, as I *follow* the example of *Christ* (1 Corinthians 11:1).

6) **Posturing humility and compassion through equality:** Be *like-minded*, having the *same love*, being one in *spirit* and *purpose.* Do nothing out of selfish ambition or vain conceit, but in **humility,** consider others *better than yourselves.* Each of you should look not only to your *own interest*, but the interest of *others* (2 Philippians 2:2-4).

7) **Submission to authorities:** Everyone must *submit*

himself to the governing authorities, for there is no authority except that which ***God has established.*** The authorities that ***exist*** have been ***established by God.*** Consequently, ***he who rebels*** against the authority is rebelling against what ***God has instituted,*** and those who do so ***will bring judgement*** on ***themselves*** (Romans 13:1-3).

8) **Putting on the full Armor of God Daily:** Be ***strong in the Lord*** and in ***his mighty power.*** Put on the ***full armor of God*** so that you can ***take your stand*** against the Devil's schemes. For our struggle is not against ***flesh*** and ***blood,*** but against the ***rulers***, against the ***authorities,*** against the ***powers of this dark world*** and against the ***spiritual forces of evil in the heavenly realms*** (Ephesians 6:10-12). With this in mind, ***be alert*** and always ***keep on praying*** for all the saints (Ephesians 6:18).

9) **Soldiers' commitment to the local church:** Your hearts must ***be fully*** committed to the ***Lord our God***, to live by ***His decrees*** and obey His commands, as at this time (1 Kings 8:61). To the faithful you show yourself faithful, to the blameless you show yourself blameless (2 Samuel 22:26). Soldiers ***first commitment*** is to their ***faith, family,*** and ***country.*** Pastors are our church legislators, together with the board members, elders and deacon. They are the ***policymakers*** and represent a congress. *(See the example at the back of this book.)*

10) **Nazarenes influence others into accomplishing the task:** Command and teach these things. Do not let ***anyone*** look down at you because you are young, but ***set the example*** for the believers in ***speech***, in ***life***, in

love, in *faith* and in *purity* (1 Timothy 4:11-12). ***Obey*** your leaders and submit to their authority. They keep watch over you as men who must give an account. ***Obey*** them so that their work will be joy, not a burden, for that would be of no advantage to you (Hebrews 13:17). ***Orderliness and discipline*** in the crop are ***essential and imperative.***

11) **Nazarenes are Christian Veterans, Present Day Saints, and Citizen Servant Soldiers:** We are ***sons and daughters of liberty.*** Our soldiery exemplifies ***ethical conduct and practices*** in accordance with the ***rules and standards*** of elders and deacons (1 Timothy 3: 1-13). We are a ***noble*** generation of men and women. We stay the course for the cause of Christ ***so that He may dwell in our hearts through faith.*** I pray that you, being ***rooted*** and ***established*** in love (Ephesians 3:17).

12) **Nazarenes set the pace:** It was He who gave some to be ***apostles,*** some to be ***prophets,*** some to be ***pastors,***and ***teachers***, to prepare God's people for the ***works of service***, so that the ***body of Christ*** may be built up until we all reach a place of ***unity in the faith*** and in the knowledge of the ***son of God*** and ***become mature,*** attaining to the whole ***measure of the fullness of Christ*** (Ephesians 4:11-13).

These principals constitute the spiritual Nazarene combat uniform of faith. Our commonality of hope is in the promise of Christ, which took hold of us upon our oath to Him by faith through grace. We are always ladies and gentlemen, present day saints. We express honor to whom honor is due without fail.

Our salute of respect is in our courtesy to all others. We will subordinate our personal ambitions to our fellow soldiers, families and friends.

E. Lock and Load

"It is easier to question than to conquer; It is easier to be skeptical than successful" (Author Unknown).

"Everyone wishes to have truth on his side, but it is not everyone that sincerely wishes to be on the side of truth" (Richard Whitely).

"The greatest security against sin is to be shocked at its presence" (Thomas Carlyle).

Troops, "Lock and Load "! My lifestyle has been suited to this old cliche. How is that, you say? Well, I have built a routine around my wife and me. In the late evening, I check all the doors and windows to ensure they are secure. I arm the alarms on our vehicles. I also walk around the house every once in a while, to check for exterior lights to see if any bulbs are out. In the morning, I occasionally check the tires for pranks such as nails or sharp objects. I take a quick look around for odd things like my neighbor's home and vehicles. I am looking for things out of place. As for my wife, she assists me in securing all the above. When night falls, if there is last-minute shopping, I will go. I have drilled safety into my wife's head. When we walk through the parking lot, I am her personal bodyguard. I look around as we walk to the car while she is laughing and talking away. I prepare myself at all times. She deserves to have peace of mind, knowing her husband is prepared to lay down his life to rescue his princess. Safeguarding my family is the highest priority. Losing my wife would be a disaster. She is my combat partner, my soul mate, my best friend, and my lover. Just Jesus, her, and I for life! It is the call and duty of every Nazarene to safeguard their family first. Our ministry begins in our home first. Ministry outside our homes is next. This will follow a greater witness of who we are in Christ. If anyone does not know how to manage his own family, how can he take care of God's family (1 Tim 3:5)? Truth be known, Nazarene soldiers have a huge responsibility to re-invent Christian living. To be a Nazarene soldier, you desire a noble task. Here are some serious "Lock and Load" ammunition definitions for you to load straight into your heart of hearts!

The following is what you are to be as a Nazarene soldier: (*Conduct of a Nazarene Soldier*)

1) **You must be above reproach.**
2) **You must have only one wife or husband.**
3) **Temperate (self-restrained).**
4) **Self-controlled (feelings and emotions in check).**
5) **Respectable (good social standing).**
6) **Hospitable (warm and generous to guests and strangers).**
7) **Teachable (capable of being instructed).**
8) **Good reputation with outsiders (non-believers).**
9) **Must be sincere (genuine in heart).**
10) **You must keep hold of the deep truths of the faith w/ a clear conscience.**
11) **You must be tested (one under authority) approved.**

The following is what you are not to be as a Nazarene soldier: *(Conduct unbecoming of a Nazarene Soldier)*

1) **Not a drunk (habitual drinker).**

2) **Not violent (quick to anger). Be gentle.**

3) **Not quarrelsome (argumentative; contentious).**

4) **Not a lover of money (false sense of security).**

5) **Not a recent convert in a position of authority (prideful or conceited).**

6) **Not pursuing dishonest gain (crooked scales and black market).**

This is straight out of (1 Timothy 3). How does your conduct measure up? If you want to truly make a difference in the lives around you, this is who you need to look like. You, too, can be a Christian 007. This is what our character must look like. Your basic training is your firm foundation. This is the only way to keep your basic training for the rest of your life, military and civilian. Remember, we still have to exist in this flesh, though our souls have been glorified with Christ. Our flesh represents the civilian life and our life in the spirit represents our military life. We, as believers in Christ, have enlisted in the most powerful military ever in existence. Satan is the commander of all lies, deceit, and delusions. He maximizes the pleasure and minimizes the consequences of sin. As a soldier, you need to rehearse the consequences of sin and who will suffer for your treachery.

Though we live in a first-class world, we need to be on guard with a third-world experience. America the beautiful, the land of milk and honey. Our liberty is sweet because our fore-fathers sweat, tears and blood! They knew the price and not the roll of the dice as to who dies and who comes home. Only the Father knows the answer to that. Our business is to keep Christ the "King of the world." Be all "God" has called us to be. We are "Extreme Nazarene" soldiers!! Be mentally "Locked and Loaded" with character ammo. Each round of ammo could be the very round that saves you or the one you are guarding, mentoring, or married to. Lack of ammo is a lack of defensive posturing. We must posture endurance through each battle! No matter the cost! Attack the lack. The lack you have. Nothing should happen on your watch. Read this over and over, "Not on my watch!" Not on my watch! Not on my watch. What does that mean exactly, you might say? To be effective in battle, you must be prepared. Train yourself to be Godly (1 Timothy 4:7).

The cost of battle profoundly impacts the one who leads the charge. That is you. Posture means an attitude, mental or spiritual stance. We are speaking about spiritual and mental posturing. Your mind contains a mass amount of thought activity. It is a super highway of information. However, the only information worth pondering is that which is noble and good for the soul. "Be on your guard so that you may not be carried away in error of lawless men and fall from your secured position" (2 Peter 3:17). Remember to say," Not on my watch!! "Make every effort to be found spotless, blameless and at peace with Him" (2 Peter 3:14). "Therefore, my bothers, be all the more eager to make your calling and election sure. For if you do these things, you will never fall, and you will receive a rich welcome into the eternal kingdom of our Lord and Savior Jesus Christ" (2 Pet 1:10-11). Keep your thoughts Locked and Loaded.! Keep your finger on the trigger of life and your aim on the center mass of the cross of Christ.

F. Prisoner of Christ Jesus

"Where has the scripture made the rule or measure of charity" (William Law).

"We believe in a Christ like world. We can conceive of nothing better. We can be satisfied with nothing less"
(Author Unknown).

"There are times when God asks nothing of his children except silence, patience, and tears"
(Charles Seymour Robinson).

The Apostle Paul speaks to us in (Ephesians 3) about his experience as a prisoner under house arrest. He, at that time, was arrested for standing firm for Christ (Ephesians 3:12). Declares our resolve of his call for us. "In him [Christ] and through faith in Him we may approach God with freedom and confidence" (Verse 12). We have zero confidence without the blood sacrifice to cleanse us from all unrighteousness. "I ask you therefore, not to be discouraged because of my suffering for you, which is your glory" (Verse 13). The apostle did not know you and I. Yet, he asked us not to be discouraged because of his suffering. He knew then that we would know now because of his suffering about our newfound freedom. Freedom of information was not known to many generations in the past. Now revealed through the Holy Spirit in you and me. The Apostle further explains, "As a prisoner for the Lord, then, I urge you to live a life worthy of the calling you have received. Be completely humble and gentle; be patient, bearing with one another in love" (Ephesians 4:1-2).

Do you think you know what it looks like to be a prisoner of Christ Jesus? How about completely humble, gentle and as fierce as a lion. Can you fix your eyes on another brother who exemplifies these awesome characteristics? If not, look harder. I know of such a man. His name is Kini Ana. This man is from Hawaii. What does he looklike? Let's see. Can you say the perfect male Hawaiian? He is good-looking, tall, with great skin, handsome, great smile, and clean white teeth. He is very well-groomed and has a very muscular physique. You probably would not want to be on the other end of his anger. He, however, is my example of excellence in humility and gentleness. Kini has every right to flex his arms when we embrace as brothers. Not once has he ever flexed in a show of arrogance. I have known Kini for almost five years now. He has not skipped a beat. At least not on my watch. Thank you, Kini, for setting the example for us in posture and as a brother. Here is another man who has postured admirable qualities. His name is Colonel Bill Bayles. He is one of my heroes of the faith, along with his beautiful wife, Linda. Bill is a man of deepprinciple; he is completely humble and gentle.

Patience is his virtue. He showed it time and time again during field and garrison operations. As for bearing with one another in love, I was always in awe of his uncanny ability to make me feel equal to himself. That was far from the truth. He and his wife exemplified Christian grace to all. I would like to reveal other events while serving under his command. Unfortunately, it is on a need-to-know basis. It is classified. Colonel Bayles and Mrs. Bayles, you both are my heroes. Thank you for completing my career and our friendship as the highlight of my military service in Europe.

I do have another hero. She is my wonderful wife and life mate. When I think of Shari, I become a marshmallow. I start acting stupid. I love her so much. I would have never imagined my life to be so perfect until God allowed our paths to cross. She has lovingly taught me how to live by love. How to be patient, how to be gentle. She has truly stood with me in love as I grew into a man. My bride modeled the essence of each of these traits, and I became a man of character. I am who I am because she took the time to help me when I could not see past me. Shari, I will always be indebted to you for your faithfulness to me. Thank you for giving me your life and becoming my wife. There is no other gem more brilliant than you. I will wear you as my crown.

Finally, once again, I would like to thank Pastor Paul Palmer. I have dedicated this book to him. He is the father of my faith and the example I draw upon when I mentor men in all phases of life. I salute him. I shall never forget him. Ever. Pray that you may have people who will impact your life like these wonderful souls have done for me. Seek out an awesome person who imitates Jesus and imitate them.

G. Red, White and Blue

"Liberty, when it begins to take root, is a plant of rapid growth" (U.S. President George Washington).

"I like to see a man proud of the place in which he lives. I like to see a man who lives in it so that his place will be proud of him" (U.S. President Abraham Lincoln).

"You belong to your own country as you belong to your own mother"

(Edward Everett Hale).

This chapter speaks about a heritage I dearly love and hold close to my heart. Our nation's flag. It symbolizes every concept we know as liberty and grace. I learned in the military that the U.S. flag is considered a living being. It represents in living color all the reasons why all military and civilians in service to our country and countries abroad had fought, lived, and died for. This is our country's identity. As a Nazarene soldier, you need to learn that the bible is living and active (Hebrews 4:12). Our country is rich in history. America, among many other countries, have made mistakes. A price highly paid. Paid in full by those who suffered at injustice or justice for this great nation.

We are like the Israelites who had extremely short-term memories and stiff necks. How fast we forget about the price our brothers and sisters paid for us to live in freedom. Is this an old song? Yes, it is. Why have we shelved the lyrics and forgotten the tune? Because, as a people, we have forgotten the sting of a fallen member. We, as a nation, have chosen to defile the blood spilled for our liberty. We were blessed not to have taken on more casualties in the operation 'Free Iraq of Saddam Hussein.' Unfortunately, our current invasion is costing us dearly. We cry bloody murder when one soldier dies of conflict wounds, and the parents of this soldier blame our President on national television? That is ludicrous and downright shameful. If you are wearing the uniform, you are a price tag called freedom and liberty. You stake your honor right or wrong. No matter if anyone in our Congress calls our involvement in any war a mistake. Oftentimes, in battle, the only picture clear to you as a soldier is covering the life of a fellow soldier. When you raised your hand

and swore into oath, your opinion was not required. How the military was going to facilitate their use of you was a risk you agreed to honor. Conscientious objectors should never be allowed to enlist in the military. The military is not a vacation destination. The military is a place of sacrifice and privilege for those who wear the uniform.

Our families, parents, and/or spouses may have concerns for you; that is normal. When they speak out publicly against your solemn oath, that is arrogance and out of line. We may one day have to experience the life of a prisoner of war. As a prisoner of war, you may have been left behind but not forgotten. You and your buddies will only have each other and the God whom you swore to uphold in principle for your country. Your very soul existence will be tested, and your faith will be brought to the brink of all but one hope. This is when Christ carries you. You may have to carry a fellow soldier, or they may have to carry you. You may be Christ to him or her at that moment. Nothing back home or in the media will change your direr circumstance? We are left to our fixed trust and hope of mercy bestowed from him whom we are willing to die for in principle for a great nation. Your survival is a puzzle piece to a greater picture. If you are missing in the puzzle, the picture is not complete, but your mission may be.

The next time you see the Arlington National Cemetery, notice all the white crosses up in rows. They are reminders to us of the pledges made, not rows of complaints and personal opinions. As a soldier, we pledge allegiance to the flag, the United States of America, and the republic for which it stands, one nation under God, indivisible, with liberty and justice for all! Indivisible means not separated into parts. Indivisible is made of two words defining one meaning. First word is individual and second word is visible. We are the visible reflection of individual hope from sea to shining sea. I believe the writers of the pledge were Christians. The intent of the pledge was to keep in our hearts the memory of those who paid the price to keep us a great nation indivisible.

Now, let us laterally associate the colors of the United States flag with Christ. The meaning behind our flag, the red, white, and blue. Red represents hardiness and valor, the blood of our nation. Blue is for justice, vigilance, and perseverance. Our God is awesome in judgement. He helps us to persevere through trials and gives us tenacity to stand vigilant against the Devil's schemes. And white stands for purity and innocence. It is our very own national monument of soldiers past, present, and future. Jesus Christ is our purity and innocence at the cross of Calvary, at the battle of salvation for all mankind on the mount of Golgotha. A place of suffering and sacrifice our Jesus gave of his blood, pure and innocent blood, that is. Christ became a prisoner of war. A battle of eternities. God did not deliver him from the sins of the world. He did not deliver many of our veterans for the sake of destiny, America! The land of the free and the home of the brave. Christ has risen and will raise all who died for his namesake. Freedom comes with a price and we are free to live because of its principle, *one nation under GOD!* It is to our shame that we entertain foolish points of view presented by a biased media defaming American blood sold for mere viewer headcount.

We are a mighty nation. Why be so swayed by the winds of change and nonsensical rhetoric? Pray!

Chapter 3: Battlefield Operations

"A soldiers love transcends all time for country, liberty, and family" (Author Shari Childress).

"By grace you are saved through faith and that not of yourself, it is the gift of God, not of works, lest any man should boast" (Ephesians 2:8-9).

"Some people complain because God put thorns on roses, while others praise Him for putting roses among thorns" (Author unknown).

A. Knowing the Terrain

"It is not good to have zeal without knowledge, nor to be hasty and miss the way" (Proverbs 19:2). Never be in a hurry to get somewhere to wait. We must recognize our position before we ever take on more territory. Acclimate yourself to your environment. If you have everbeen in the military, you know you do not salute an officer on the battlefield. In war time scenario, the enemy searches for the leaders as prime targets. The enemy sniper hides in waiting, watching from the ridges afar. He watches carefully to know who to target first. The enemy knows if they take out the leaders mass confusion begins! We must recognize the terrain we have to enter soon. Knowing your terrain can be the difference between life and death. We must always be ready for whatever comes our way. This means being ready in and out of season.

While driving to work or coming home, what do you see?

High school kids walking home? Are you fantasizing about your thoughts? Do you see the same person at the bus stop every day and cannot wait to drive by to sneak a peek? Maybe you cannot wait to see them tomorrow too? Maybe you cannot wait to see them tomorrow, too? What about some jogger with the tight outfit? Are you winking at a co-worker from across the room? Have you recognized the terrain you are on yet? How about being excited to go to work to see the new secretary? Are you inviting a co-worker to lunch so you can innocently flirt with them? As you walk through the grocery store, what magazine did you pick up and why?

The enemy is watching whom he might have to pick off first. The terrain can get you caught by the enemy troops waiting to ambush your Christian walk. They are not waiting for innocent blood, only for the guilty. They want to make you a prisoner of your own flesh. Let us cut to the chase here. Heroes are men and women who meditate on things that are good for the soul, period! Do you have enough evidence against you to be found guilty of Christian living? "Finally, brothers, whatever is true, whatever is noble, whatever is right, whatever is pure, whatever is lovely, whatever is admirable—if anything excellent and praiseworthy-think about such things" (Philippians 4:8). You remember the cool commercial on television about the credit card. At the end of the commercial, someone says, "What is in your wallet?" I will ask you the same question, but with one word changed. "What is in your mind?"

"A sculptor once fashioned a magnificent lion out of solid stone. When asked how he had accomplished such a wonderful masterpiece, he replied, 'It was easy. All I did was to chip away everything that did not look like a lion' (Author unknown). We should all let God chip away everything in our lives that does not look like Christ! Quite the platitude of preponderance. We should keep our minds off of anything that could make us look and act inappropriately. We can keep our eyes on the terrain and be innocent of false accusations from Satan. Satan is the enemy of God and man. We must orientate our minds to the bigger picture of life. Life in the Spirit is the heart of God. The military definition of a map is a picture of a portion of the earth's surface drawn to scale on a map. My definition of the Bible map is a picture of a portion of God's perfect plan drawn to scale on a map on earth. The map of life as is and what is to come! The Holy Spirit is our compass and absolute true north in Christ Jesus. Our truth, in some ways, has been developed by men and influenced by Satan. The sins of this world point to the false north. Like reading your compass, the same is true when understanding your direction as we walk through life in all types of terrain. The word of God always points to Christ. Old maps and new maps. (Old testament and new testament).

The military compass is an amazing instrument. It has gotten me out of some close calls. However, there is something you need to know about the compass. Your magnetic compass can be influenced by metal on a belt buckle to large metal objects in close range. Our truth, as we know, is also influenced by other spheres around us. Evil darkness can blind us. Magnetic north is not as accurate as you may have thought. The following is a clear understanding of magnetic north and the North Pole polarity. "One thing to remember: a compass does not really point to true north, except by coincidence in some areas. The compass needle is attracted by magnetic force, which varies in different parts of the world and is constantly changing. When you read north on a compass, you are really reading the direction of the magnetic north pole. A diagram in the map margin will show the difference (declination) at the center of the map between compass north (magnetic north indicated by the MN symbol) and true north (polar north indicated by the "star" symbol). This diagram also provides the declination between true north and the orientation of the Universal Transverse Mercator (UTM) grid north (indicated by the GN symbol). The declination diagram is only representational, and true values of the angles of declination should be taken from the numbers provided rather than from the directional lines. Because the magnetic declination is computed at the time the map is made, and because the position of magnetic north is constantly changing, the declination factor provided on any given map may not be current" (National Geomagnetic Information Center).

Information we receive on a daily basis reminds me of grid coordinates and declination lines on the map of life. What we are told through the media, co-workers, books, wives' tales, and just bad information offsets the truth. From hearsay or warped gossip, how we should live is off-setting the physical true north. Our examples come from our home life experience, and often it is hard to break the old habits. As we read the map of life in the flesh, our understanding of direction is misguided. As time goes by, our understanding deteriorates. As we get older, without the map of life in the spirit, we are in a living hell. God's map of life never changes and always points to the true north, Christ—our absolute truth. Grid coordinates show intersecting lines at a right angle. This makes up a system of measured distance and declination of bending, sloping, or moving downward slopes. This causes a deterioration in measure. Both are used to define direction on a map. Grid coordinates stay the same on maps. Remember as you have read earlier, magnetic declination changes with time and needs to be recalculated with each new map. Something similar to finding yourself at a dead end in the seasons of your life.

Time changes us all. As we process the world's truths, we automatically are in declination even if our grid coordinate is accurate. Accurate, as in, they represent levels of maturity and stations in life. As we walk through life, grids specify a specific measurement of accomplishment in life. For example, some of us are lawyers, doctors, and law enforcement officers. These titles do not describe who we are. They are simply a place on the map of life (as a grid). Our lifestyle (as in declination) reveals the direction in life we have taken. The world's life maps are scaled one way. It is the wrong direction. To lead us astray, in blind flesh and emotional oblivion. We have to orientate ourselves to the gospel map, as we would orientate ourselves on a map, to discover our true north. Jesus is our true north. In order to understand in which direction we are going in our lives, we must determine our bearing. According to map reading instructions, the following will best describe how to determine your directions. When reading a map, you have to determine a few things. To determine the direction, or bearing, from one point to another, you need a compass as well as a map. "Most compasses are marked with the four cardinal points—north, east, south, and west—but some are marked additionally with the number of degrees in a circle (360: north is 0 or 360, east is 90, south is 180, and west is 270). Both kinds are easy to use with a little practice" (National Geomagnetic Information Center).

Practice does keep you on course. I have heard, "No matter how far you travel toward the west, in order to travel east, just turn around and you are in an easterly direction" (Author unknown). East is not a distance; it's a direction. As we travel, especially as soldiers, we go nowhere without first navigating our course. A Nazarene soldier will spend the rest of their life planning and formulating a vision for their family. We have to be expert troubleshooters for life issues. "Whatever you have learned or received or heard from me-put it into practice. And the God of peace will be with you" (Philippians 4:9). "The shortest distance between a problem and a solution is the distance between your knees and the floor. The one who kneels to the Lord can stand up to anything." (Author unknown).

Navigating our course is to understand the terrain you are in and recognize the best course of travel. There is a lot of troubleshooting and navigating through a world full of jungle lies and desert terrain booby traps. I have a rule of thumb for my personal decision-making when life's travels bring me to a difficult crossroads. I examine the information and remind myself that the easy way is always the wrong way. The easy way means you pay later while borrowing time as credit. Credit means pleasure with delayed payment. The hard way, you pay as you go; all debts are even. Later is always wrong; it leads to hidden penalties and now keeps you idly mischievous. I've found that traveling from hilltop to hilltop without the valley experiences keeps you from ever maturing in Christ. It is living a lie. "[We must] walk through the valley of the shadow of death and fear no evil, for Christ is with us" (Psalms 23:4) (Emphasizes added) Proverbs 1: 2-3, 7 says it best: 2-3 "For obtaining wisdom and discipline; for understanding words of insight; for acquiring a disciplined life, doing what is right and just and fair" (Proverbs 1:2- 3). "The fear of the Lord is the beginning of Knowledge, but fools despise wisdom and discipline" (Proverbs 1:7).

We are soldiers of the cross of Christ. As we conquer one hilltop, we must climb the next one in order to capture its magnificent view. If it were not for mountains, we would not learn how to climb. Each mountain has a name, and every valley has its battle. We should all journal our experiences. This is the legacy we will leave behind from generation to generation. Does anyone in your family know the history of your family and where everyone has come from? Where are the records of life?

B. Forward Observer

"I am only one, but I am one. I cannot do everything, but I can do something. And that which I can do, by grace of God, I will do" (Dwight L. Moody).

"There is not freedom on earth or in any star for those who deny freedom to others" (Elbert Hubbard).

"Your sin will not impede upon the character of Christ; though it will assassinate your identity" (Adam P. Childress).

Soldiers understand "forward observer" to mean sending an advance mission to survey the territory and terrain for enemy information. A spiritual concept of "forward observer" is to recognize enemy advancement and prepare to engage the enemy with our earthly authority. As in the beginning, in the garden, Adam had authority over all things on earth. "God blessed them and said to them, be fruitful and increase in number; fill the earth and subdue it. Rule over the fish of the sea and the birds of the air and over every living thing that moves on the ground" (Geneses 1:28). Unfortunately, Adam was with Eve and did not observe what was taking place right before his eyes. "And the Lord God commanded the man, "You are free to eat from any tree in the garden; but you must not eat from the tree of knowledge of good and evil, for when you eat of it you will surely die" (Geneses 2:16). Why did Adam not step in and say something? Why did he just stand there? Why did he not tell Eve to stop talking to this crafty serpent? Maybe Adam was caught up looking at Eve's booby traps. Men get caught in the boo bee trap all the time. Adam was in charge of all things that moved on earth (Gen 1:28). He was the ruler and possessed the authority. Adam was no slow Joe. He named every beast, bird, and livestock God created. Plus, when God created each living thing, he brought it to Adam to name (Gen 2:19-20). Adam and God were relating as do you and your sons. God commanded Adam not to eat from the tree, the very tree that would kill him if he ate from it! Why did he not stop Eve from biting into the apple? This is an age-old question asked of men throughout the years. Why do men just stand by and keep their mouths shut?

My good friend was quoted as saying, "When a nation goes to war, they do not send their wives into combat. So why does the church have more women in the ranks of combat than men" (Author Kini Ana). The future maybe a time you will wish you would have done what you are not doing now. "Knowledge comes from taking things apart; analysis. Wisdom comes from putting things back together" (Author John Morrison). Do not expect anything original from an echo. Postponed obedience is disobedience. Do not put off something for tomorrow, what you can accomplish today. Basically, be different and unusual. It is time to forward observe and change the way we charge toward the world. Be an uncommon soldier! Satan stole Adam's authority over the dominion of the earth. Jesus Christ stripped it out of the hand of Satan by the work of the cross and empowered us by the Holy Spirit to be back in authority once again. Amen! We are in charge again! The earth is ours and we are to subdue it and rule over it as originally planned in the beginning. We must take charge of our duties and get back into action. The wishbone will never replace the backbone. We need to stand up, not stand by, as Adam did. We need to say something when we know it is not right. We need to butt in on conversations when the truth has been defiled. We need to take notice of all aspects of our wives, children, families, friends, and workplaces. Stop slacking off our responsibilities on our wives and others. We must lead the way in all things or can we blame our help mates on Judgement Day, like Adam? How long will we sit around and eat the fat of the Lamb of God? We bask in the glory and never raise a finger to dress in righteousness. Stand up! How long will we continue to drink from the same cup as Adam?

C. Posturing Valor

"Yet, Freedom! Yet thy banner, torn, but flying, streams like the thunderstorm against the wind" (Lord Byron).

"Great men are they who see that spiritual is stronger than any material force; that thoughts rule the world" (Ralph Waldo Emerson).

"Life is a great big canvas and you should throw all the paint on it that you can" (Danny Kaye).

When we consider the word marriage, we do not associate its theme with a military operation. G.I. stands for "government issue." If the government wanted for you to have a wife, they would have issued you one? Ha Haa Haaa!!! (Duck and cover). This chapter really does speak mostly to married men. I say we have the greatest tactical positioning ever faced in a man's life. It takes pure valor to face the world at large while being a young married couple, a re-married couple, or a couple coming from ridiculous backgrounds. Nothing can get you ready to take on such collateral damage for the rest of your natural life. Truthfully, marriage is a great place to level the battlefield and start anew.

Valor means to be bold and determined in the face of battle or danger. Getting married with a truckload of dirty laundry takes a man of great valor. As men, we must be bold thinkers when it comes to our husbandship. We must go into strict training and rehearse our role in the relationship with our wives, children, community, workplace, and especially the church. To posture valor, we must become heroes to our families and communities. Operation Valor is a plan to turn the hearts of men. We want to turn the hearts from lazy, laid back, let our wives man the responsibilities attitude and wash away our ungrateful, disorientated, and arrogant bench-warmer lifestyles. Maybe we are grateful. We cannot seem to break our laziness, no matter how often our wives remind us and beg us to help. Our expectation is to be served and chill out because we are men. We put in our eight or ten hours at the job and the rest of our awake time is sleepwalking to the television. Wrong stupid!! Slap yourself upside the head and get real. Maybe someone should take you out back and kick some Jesus in you. I bet you need some old-fashioned laying of hands on you in a rapid motion until you see straight. We will still love you even after we cast the sleepwalking idiot out of you. Men, we need to see the wrong we have done. Some of our fathers taught us nothing, and now we need to change our destiny. We need to have a desire to leave our sons and daughters a new legacy!! Heroes leave legacies; zeroes leave tragedies.

I am a true believer that when you are going in the wrong direction, stop! Regroup, turn around and think differently. Change direction. Change your habits. Turn your life upside down and make new standards for yourself. If you sleep in, wake up earlier! Are you falling asleep when you read at night? Read in the morning! Does your wife always remind you to help out? Please, for the sake of all other men, leave yourself a note in three places to remind yourself to do it. You must change for yourself and your familiy's benefit. Does your wife ask you where you would like to eat on date night? Do you say, "I do not care, wherever you want to, honey?" Then a fight ensues, and after ten volleys, no one cares where anyone wants to eat. You cannot decide? Stop having your wife ask you where you would like to eat. The majority of the time you should give her at least two choices and let her pick it. If she cannot decide, then you choose one and stick to it. Even if she complains later about how bad it was, stand up. Stand up in gentleness with authority. Valor means boldness or determination while facing great danger, as in battle, remember?

Most of the time, men do not want to rock the boat in fear they could anger their wives. We do not want to make waves. We do not want to challenge the moment. I say, wake up. Get involved. Be a part of the equation and start living in your role as a husband! Rock the boat and splash some water around. If you fall into the water, you know how to swim. Our wives crave loving leadership. Use the same tenacity you used to rescue your beauty from the single life and lead her as you are one in Christ. She is your beauty you have rescued. Treat her like your princess and she will allow you to govern the kingdom of your home. This is something you will have to earn, not take, or you will drown in the sea of pride. "Deep in his heart, every man long for a battle to fight, an adventure to live, and a beauty to rescue" (Author John Eldredge). It is time we men trade in our panties for boxers, step into the ring of life, and win some rounds for our families. Boldness is our lead and being a husband is our right to cover our families by being first on the battlefield. That is the battle to fight.

Two days ago, I and some from our men's group drove down to Phoenix, Arizona, to attend Promise Keepers. I will be transparent with you, I was not super excited to go, only because I am already fired up as it is. Well, I realized a tremendous revelation on this trip. I realized; it is not PK's job to get us fired up. It was the mere traveling to and from PK that we bonded beyond the message delivered at the conference. If it were not for PK, we would have never experienced the message in the travel to and from. What we had expected to get from the conference and what we received traveling together was unparalleled. We shared eight hours of adventure, talking about personal feelings, losses, gains, failures, triumphs, and defeats. We found out how similar we were to each other and are not alone in the adventure of life. Exactly what Satan did not want us to figure out. Some men spoke of feeling absolutely alone in a stadium of 18,000. One spoke of the loss of his wife to cancer. She was his sweetheart and best friend. Another had spoken of feeling lost and unreachable. He was in a stadium with hundreds of men around him. And yet another was overwhelmed to be surrounded by all the praise and power of 18,000 men singing, "Holy is the Lamb." I was among some of the most transparent and genuine men I had ever been with. We experienced the adventure of a road warrior, with camaraderie like never before. Time spent with other men has brought a clearer meaning to scripture we commonly quote, "As iron sharpens iron, so one man sharpens another" (Prov 27:17).

We are the swordsmen of God's word. Let us be men who develop and mold our character to bless our marriages. Let us change the destiny of our marriages not by what we say but by what we do. Stop talking, put your faith where your mouth is and start walking. All for the One.

D. PTSD (Post Traumatic Stress Disorder)

"More than an end to war, we want an end to the beginnings of all wars" (Franklin D. Roosevelt, 32nd President).

"I only regret that I have but one life to lose for my country" (Nathan Hale, soldier).

"I leave you, hoping that the lamp of liberty will burn in your bosoms, until there shall no longer be a doubt that all men are created equal" (Abraham Lincoln 16th President).

According to the "Department of Veteran Affairs," the following is the definition of Post-traumatic stress disorder (PTSD) [in part, not whole]: "Post-Traumatic Stress Disorder is a psychiatric disorder that can occur following the experience or witnessing of life-threatening events, such as military combat, natural disasters, terrorist incidents, serious accidents, abuse, 'sexual, physical, emotional, and/or ritual,' and violent personal assaults like rape. People who have suffered from PTSD often relive the experiences through nightmares and flashbacks, have difficulty sleeping, and feel detached or estranged. These symptoms can be severe enough and last long enough to significantly impair the persons' daily life.)

To approach this subject, we know it is titanic and overwhelming, I am going to do my best to slice and dice a sense of clarity to further healing in the lives of those who have been bitten by the lie of the enemy. The venom produced by the bite is the cause of PTSDs in life's arena. First, allow me to say, the casualty report is extremely high and unacceptable in our society. There are five areas where we can identify a failure to adapt and follow through in our God-given capacity. Those who have experienced PTSD may think someone permitted them to express their flashbacks through violence and anger. The answer to that is no and you are wrong for thinking it. Let us get back to the five areas to identify failure:

1. Our childhood experiences
2. Our adolescents (puberty)
3. Toxic parenting
4. Self-inflicted addictions.

Unfortunately, people are thrown into a lifetime of personal tail-spin trauma. After years of spinning out of incomprehensible trauma, you find yourself walking up the wreckage of your life. You are dumbfounded and perplexed, wondering how you got there. You are found to be highly dysfunctional and the poison has now begun its crippling effects on your nervous system. Your personality has formed psychosomatic symptoms. Finally, you find yourself with uncontrollable mood swings, from Earth to the moon and back. Doctors call this a bipolar disorder. Symptoms of bipolar disorder, according to (My DNA.Com), are defined as, [in short order form], "bi-polar disorder causes dramatic mood swings from 'High' and/or irritable to sad and hopeless, and then back again, often with periods of normal moods in between. Severe changes in energy and behavior go along with these changes in moods. Our mental condition (not including those with medical conditions) often reflects our decision-making process or lack of."

Our standard of life leads us into barrages of worldly distractions if we doubt God's word. America has never been more doubtful of truth in Christ in recent history. Bipolar may be a fallout effect due to extreme levels of satanic influences upon the family unit for decades. Depression begins to trigger PTSD? We truly live on the front line of the battle. In Genesis, the serpent caused Eve and Adam to doubt God's word, and they both had a bipolar moment. How psychotic to think for a moment that you would want to be like God? Satan knew already that God had made man in His image already. That is the only way he could think of something so farfetched as to say, "For God knows when you eat of it, your eyes will be opened and you will be like God, knowing good and evil" (Gen 3:5). In addition, Adam and Eve both knew the difference between good and evil. You would have to know the concept of good and evil in order to entertain a contradictive question of God's law. God made them with a mature mind and the ability to care for the greatest garden ever created. Eve was a suitable helper. Sex was definitely in the equation. "The man and his wife were both naked, and they felt no shame" (Genesis 2:25). To imply shame is to have a consciousness of regret. When a law abounds so does judgement. They simply made the wrong decision out of a careless moment. They had a serious personal tailspin of consequence and trauma. It is moments like this in our lives when our mental faculties receive the greatest damage of all. You lose it!!! Pressure in your head begins to chemically change and you experience anxiety. Unchecked prolonged anxiety could lead to mental health issues. Please understand that what you are reading is not sound medical advice, opinion, and/or fact. What you are reading is a theory only. This information is a healthy way of understanding an idea of how to work through and identify trauma. After identifying the trauma, we come to post-trauma. Finding a source is greater than treating the symptoms.

Let us look back at the beginning of the chapter when we spoke about five areas when our ability to adapt to life fails. I mentioned our childhood experiences. As children, we absorb information faster than a high-speed computer. However, we are influenced by anything and everything around us. As we begin to assimilate a personality, we find that the encouragement or discouragement of daily functions and activities determines our destiny to make decisions for the rest of our lives. Secondly, in the line of adapting to life, when we reach adolescence, our personality has developed in one of two ways. You are either an introvert or an extravert. Why? First, let us look at an introverted person. An introverted person is characterized as one who is interested primarily in one's own thoughts and feelings, a private personality. Introverted personalities exist well in a more isolated environment. They are also known to be quiet and even shy.

Now, an extroverted person. An extroverted personality is someone who is interested in the exterior conditions of one's life. Extroverted people are more connected to people, places, and things. This person is sociable in personality. This gives a small insight into a bipolar personality, though they are not extreme in the natural sense. There is continuity in understanding an opposite connection between a positive and negative characteristic. Here, our mental pathways are developing acutely. Nerves are fused permanently by chemicals in our brain used to channel expression by way of a nerve control center. The process of expression is an electrical impulse (wave sensory) traveling through a designed chemical to communicate to a particular muscle, gland, or other nerve cells in your nerve command center. Sometimes, genetics play a larger part in the bipolar condition. I happen to believe PTSD has its hand in the misfiring of chemicals due to the hurtful conditions we have experienced in our lives. The list is too long to write here and identify every area we have failed to adapt in our God-given capacity. The venom of the serpent is quite effective on the unexpected. We have an antidote called the blood transfusion of Christ Jesus. We must walk in the healing power of Jesus.

Furthermore, we have yet to talk about number three, toxic parents, and number four, self-inflicted addiction. Both of these two subjects are synonymous. Toxic parents cause the largest hurdles in life. This has led many of us straight into self-inflicted addictions. We tend to live with poor self-esteem or just a straight-out rebellious attitude. We drive our bodies into sexual slavery and prostitute ourselves to the fastest sexual release. We are extremely addicted to self-gratification and will trade our natural relationships for unnatural ones. Now that is what I call "being pimped by the devil!" Nothing like being put on the corner of a secret sin and pulling your shift of "prostitution." We are caught in the trap of masturbation, pornographic videos, magazines, fantasies, burning lust, and drugs to stay in denial. All the while, that demon pumps his venom in your veins. This could cause serious mental damage and illusions. Some fall to paranoia. What trauma of memories to suppress or to be healed of? This may be a 'cross scare' for you to bear all your life, not because God put it there. You chose the wrong road to travel on and the Devil ambushed you in plain view. Thank God you trusted in Jesus Christ! You are now cleansed and free from additions bond over you. You may have those reoccurring urges. Those are what I call cross scares. When you cross over from darkness into the light, the former wounds have left their scares. Your cross scares are your greatest testimony of who you were and who you are! You are a shining star! Bear your cross with honor and dignity; you are saved by GRACE! "Then he said to them all: If anyone would come after me, he must deny himself and take up his cross daily and follow me. For whoever wants to save his life will lose it, but whoever loses his life for me will save it. What good is it for a man to gain the whole world, and yet lose or forfeit his very self (soul). If anyone is ashamed of me and my words, the Son of Man will be ashamed of him when he comes in his glory and in his glory of the Father and the Holy angels" (Luke 9:23-26). You have nothing to be ashamed of. Calling all sinners, calling all sinners, retreat to the cross. Retreat, pick up your cross daily, and deny the lie of the evil one. Deny yourself with draws of burning lust, even when it hurts. Be not ashamed; we all fall down. Back up, start on your knees, hands together and surrender to grace. Measure your sins between falls. Do not give up. If you walk away now, you will walk away from everything. The fastest way to turn evil around is to spell live. Now start living Christ.

E. Knowing the Objective

"Success is not perfection; success is slightly above average" (Unknown).

"Only America makes you feel that everybody wants to be like you. That's what success is: everybody wants to be like you" (Ornette Coleman).

"Whatever America hopes to bring to pass in this world must first come to pass in the heart of America" (Dwight D Eisenhower 34th President).

In the middle of "Desert Shield," our supply lines were getting washed away as the night poured water like a broken dam. No signs of trails anywhere and the enemy was hidden all around us. My leader had forgotten to take a grid coordinate and a back azimuth two days earlier. We were in quite a fix now. Our objective was clear. Keep the front line ammoed up and the tanks stocked hot and heavy! So, in the midst of our moment of absolute blunder, I remembered taking a back azimuth. I was ensuring the accuracy of my own compass just in case I was separated from my crew. I had also backed it into my rucksack some extra MREs. Well, I became the hero that night. I was able to guide us through enemy territory and back to our supply points with the navigation of my compass. Only God knew I was going to need that compass.

The compass we use to orient ourselves to a map can equally be said of the Holy Spirit of God in our lives. The Holy Spirit orientates us to the map of life, our Bible. The Bible is the map of life and points directly to Christ, our true north. The Spirit of God points us to the truest north ever known to man. I know we covered this already. Repetition is the key to learning. We accept the truth of God's word; we have living in us the Holy Spirit of God in Christ Jesus. "In the beginning was the Word, and the Word was with God, and the Word was God in the beginning. He was with God in the beginning. Through him all things were made; without him nothing was made" (John 1:1-2). How was the Earth created? God said, "Let there be light." Just by the spoken Word of God. Who is the Word? Jesus is the word. "The word became flesh [Jesus] and made his dwelling among us" (John 1:14). Jesus, the Word of life, created all things. He then became flesh of our flesh. He is God in the flesh. He dwelled with us tiny fleshlings? How can it be?

Christ, who created everything in existence, put himself below his own creation. He also put himself under the submission of God. Jesus proves His point by dying on the cross. He arises three days later as He promised. Then He ascended into heaven and His Holy Spirit descended to fill our hearts with joy. He knew we could obtain freedom from sin only through His plan of "voluntary faith initiative." We need to know the objective and execute our voluntary faith initiative. We have the Spirit of Christ. We have the Word of life. We have the double-edged sword of the spirit. All three in one, like the trinity of God. One side of the double-edged sword is the Spirit and the other edge is the word of life. "Spirit and Word = Sword." See, Spirit and Word are synonymous. When the Spirit and the word are used together, that is the sword in action. In order to wield the sword, we must speak in the authority of the Spirit and Word. Spirit of Christ is the in-living host within us. Christ is living in you. He is recreating you from the inside out. Are you living for Christ with your insides out? Is He living in you, guiding you like a compass in the Word of life? Is he training you to wield His double-edged sword of power and mercy? I believe the very soul of God is Jesus Christ. I believe the very soul of Jesus is the double-edged sword. Every man born of a woman is born with a soul. Jesus was born of the virgin Mary and he, too, had a soul. He was God and man. One hundred percent flesh, soul, and spirit. He is all three in one. He is the living trinity for all in existence.

What did His soul look like? Well, we are made in the image of the trinity (God, Word, and Spirit). "Let us make man in our image, in our likeness" (Geneses 1:26). God spoke and His word (Jesus) being the soul of God Himself. His word became flesh. His soul covered in flesh was the image of the father. Here we have Jesus Christ the only perfect soul ever generated into flesh. Jesus said, "when you see me, you have seen the father "(John 14:9). The words spoken out of the mouth of Christ are the same words that created all things. The soul of Jesus is his word. The words He had spoken are the actions of a double-edged sword. "And out of His mouth came a sharp Double-Edged Sword." (Rev 1:16). I believe the Holy Spirit is the embodiment of God's amazing grace. The Holy Spirit is our comforter. God speaks to us with grace and mercy through the work of His son, our Savior. Wow, is this over-the-edge thinking? Christ lives in you; you have the same authority to do supernatural conquest!! You have, in you, the same power of the sword of the Spirit. Back in the days when the Apostle Paul was writing in Rome, he used an insignia of a Bible laid open on top of a double-edged sword. Do you know what he called that in Latin? He called it "Spiritus Gladius," which means sword of the Spirit! When you open your mouth, do you speak life or death? You and I are ambassadors of the living God. We are powerhouses for Jesus. We have the ability to speak through darkness as if we were walking through time as invisible warriors. We are the warriors of light travel. We walk by faith through grace with the sword of the spirit and lead the captives free!!

Spiritus Gladius!

F. Communications, Command and Control of Intelligence (C3I)

"For Every pound of learning a person has, he needs ten pounds of common sense to know how to use it" (Persian Proverb).

"Do you know that if you yield yourself to anyone as obedient slaves, you are slaves of the one whom you obey, either of sin, which leads to death, or of obedience, which leads to righteousness" (Romans 6:16).

"For time has come for the judgement to begin with the household of God; and if it begins with us, what will be the end of those who do not obey the gospel of God" (1 Peter 4:17).

C3I Deals with the swift control of intelligence. Satellite signals, computer technology, and photo surveillance provide information on enemy travel and country movement. This conduit of intelligence (all on a need-to-know basis, top secret) is pumped into a command structure. All details are sifted, raked, and peeled apart for accuracy. The information is then distributed to officials, general staff, field commanders, and down the chain of command as directed. Communication is the key to any and all processes of leadership. Leadership from the top of the food chain to the very last man standing. As a young

NCO (Non-commissioned officer), I learned to be an effective communicator due to the poor leaders I had to follow. There are two ways to handle poor leadership. One, follow in their footsteps and learn nothing. Two, train yourself to disregard the information and be an effective leader. Not a defective leader. This is a good school of thought, worthy of repeating to others. You can always learn from any leader, good or bad; you must choose to repeat or delete information. As a leader, you are held to a higher standard, which is no joke. God will reckon with the leaders first.

Look it up, soldier! It is in His word. I have always enjoyed using acronyms to assist my learning capacity. For example, leadership is twofold and the following is a definition: Leadership to others and to one's self. (Two-fold)

Meaning of Leadership

(To others)

L—loves even when you have been hurt, when it is unfair, or when they are wrong.

E—evaluates character strengths and weaknesses without judging people.

A—addresses a conflict immediately, lovingly, corrects, or asks for forgiveness.

D—delegates others in their giftings, talents, ministries, and missions.

E—elevates others in truth, motivating the hearts of fellow soldiers.

R—responds to others, slow to anger, patient and not reactive to pressures.

(To one's self)

S—sanctified in the deep truths of God's Word and treasures his purity.

H—humbled in posture, gentle in greatness mixed with fear unto the Lord God.

I—intercedes in prayer for his family, church, neighbor, nation, and world.

P—purposes his faith while rehearsing the consequences of sin and stays accountable to a mature friend.

This intelligence you receive is of high priority and must be guarded with your life at all times. As Christian soldiers, C3I means Colossians 3:1. "Since, then, you have been raised with Christ, set your hearts on things above, where Christ is seated at the right hand of God" (Colossians3:1). Communications, command and control of intelligence need to be a complete focus on whom we serve. When we serve all people, not just people in the body of Christ, but outsiders too. We need to practice remembering the names of acquaintances and their family members. Truly listening to their thoughts and asking them at a later date how the situation is or if that someone is feeling better. Care is spelled T-I-M-E. Something we do not always have a lot of.

Your command of Bible theory is fundamental to how you communicate your philosophy of life within the scriptures. What I mean is how you live your life must measure up to how you act and speak. Not everyone will memorize more than three favorite scriptures in a lifetime. So, you must read the word daily to grasp an understanding of absolute truths and base your lifestyle on the theory. You may not be able to quote many memory scriptures. Does your life and the words you speak exemplify the living proof of your testimony? I know of countless brothers and sisters in the Lord who can quote scripture until sunset. Some are also the ones who have trouble keeping a job for more than six months. Some have trouble disciplining their children. Some are just downright immature in their faith. It is not how much memorization we accomplish. It is what we do with what we have internalized as truth.

A simple equation for you in keeping with a good philosophy or theory. When you fail in a decision, you must learn to measure your maturity by the depth of your fall. See, if you say, "I am going to stop cursing." Two days later, you get mad and say a bad word. You are only two days mature in your decision-making process. At this time, you ask for forgiveness and repent of your failure. You decide not to curse again. Now it has been two weeks. Again, you continue to measure failure to become mature in all decisions. (Self-denial is the key to maturity.) Finally, you have not cursed in two years and are going stronger than ever. You have evidence of maturity and your decisions measure up with what lives in your heart. What lives in your heart is God's unfailing love and absolute truths. Store up God's word in your heart and be true to your decisions. You will become rock solid mature. Let your yes be yes and your no be no. This is your commitment to faith in action. No one can lead if they are immature and indecisive. Everyone around you is counting on the information you are disseminating. Your leadership skills cannot be counterfeit. Everyone knows a fake when they see it at work. We see it in sports. The whole world can see it on the Hollywood report cards. People prefer to be led by a genuine, caring person. They are willing to follow a person who may not have the answers to all of life's snags as long as they know that person really cares about them. Be sure to control information as you get or give it. Misunderstandings can be hurtful and damaging if not guarded or confronted. Confront them quickly, with boldness and gentleness. Correct in love at all times. Correct and admonish with grace and serious diplomacy. You are an ambassador of the most exalted God. Be prepared to humble yourself at a moment's notice. If you are even a little bit guilty, own it quickly. As a leader, you are an example. Your attitude should be, "imitate me as I imitate Christ." "Therefore, as God's chosen people holy and dearly loved, clothe yourselves with compassion, kindness, humility, gentleness and patience" (Colossians 3:12). Leaders are the first on the battleground and the last foot off the battlefield. Troops first and leaders last. We will have it no other way.

Chapter 4: My Testimony

Born in 1966 in Harvey, Illinois (South Chicago). That very year, my mother, sister, and I were caught in the blizzard of 1966 in Chicago. We would have starved to death if my mother had not used serious survival skills to make pancakes out of flour and water for months. That was a close call. My parents' marriage was hitting major lows. My father, who spent three tours in Vietnam, was by this time quit a different person altogether. After some brutal encounters, my parents split. What a beginning! My mother left my father and three kids in his care at Ft. Richie, Maryland. He did not know how to care for a six-year-old girl, a five-year-old boy, and a one-year-old boy. We were a handful for a Vietnam vet with serious battle scars.

In 1972, for some time, maybe even a year, we were cared for by a temporary foster family. She was a large African American woman we called Momma Brooks. She commanded attention and when she said to do something, you had better move with swiftness. If you did not, you could be in great danger in a good way. You will respect Momma Brooks because she loved you with everything in this world. "Comes hear, boyee," she'd say to me. "What are you cry'en about?" I would lower my head and tell her all about a little five-year-old boy's problems. She would say, "Comes to Momma Brooks, baby. All you needs is a little shugar to be awe'right, honey boyee." She would press my head against her chest. Momma Brooks held me until it all went away. I still miss those hugs and her singing. Momma Brooks will be in my heart for eternity. After a time, my father came and took us away. I never saw Momma Brooks ever again.

In 1973, we were pawned off to a more permanent foster family. Life was not the same in this foster home. After two and a half years of sexual, physical, and mental abuse, we were a mess. While living at the foster home, I learned to work hard and long hours. Our chores included: feeding cows, shoveling manure, feeding livestock, bailing hay, stacking hay, and weeding a garden. Going to school was, for me, the fondest time. I was very fond of Sister Carol, who became my godmother. She really loved me. She treated me with lots of love. While attending a Catholic school, we always started our school days in prayer in the chapel. That is when I first felt the Lord in my heart of hearts. I would sing from the top of my voice in the chapel and loved to hear my voice echo off the ceiling. The smell of incense in the area and the priest speaking all those holy chants made me feel safe. Safe was relative as the abuse grew worse at the foster home. The chapel became my safe zone. Day in and day out, fighting ensued. The mental abuse increased; the perverted night games were unbearable for my sister and me.

In the meantime, our little minds were shutting down, and we ate like animals. We did not use forks, knives, or spoons all the time. We ate with our hands. Some days, we acted totally normal and other days like a wild pack of dogs. After a time, the state gave us a battery aptitude test to evaluate us. I was certified as mentally retarded. Now, the abuse stepped up a notch. The "retarded boy" did not understand what was going on. (I do want to make something completely clear: the foster parents had nothing to do with the sexual abuse.) Well, not everyone was convinced that I was retarded. Sister Carol was not happy with their assessments. Many years later, I found a letter she had written to my grandfather. She had stated that she had spent many hours with me and could assure anyone, I was not retarded.

As time passed, the sexual predator would sneak into my bed and begin the abuse. As I lay there, I remembered an angel sitting close to me and talking to me while things were being done to me. When I saw the angel, I had no fear, shame, or pain. The angel knew what was happening to me was wrong. The angel and I would talk about swimming holes, night crawlers, fireflies, and our favorite candy after the abuse had taken place. He always liked the same things I did. When I would laugh, he would laugh. When I had cried, he cried too. As I look back in my mind's eye, I never saw his mouth. I could hear his voice. Time went by fast and when the angel left, I was fast asleep. He never failed to show up. He always knew when I needed him most. The abuse began to slack off. I believe it was due to the news of my grandfather's timely letters arriving at the foster home.

1974, my grandfather, who resided in Italy, had written letters to every state senator and congressman in America. (I come from a long line of mighty men, starting with my grandfather.)

1975, the battle for the three children began. By 1976, my grandfather, my mother, and her new soon-to-be-husband won the battle. [Praise God.] Finally, we loaded up in the brand-new Grand Prix they showed up in and headed to Colorado Springs, Colorado. A new family. All the dirty laundry (abuse we endured). Two and a half years passed and we mixed with our new three brothers from my new father's divorce. Now, talk about total and utter dysfunction. My new father was unequipped to take on a mission from Mars; who could be? My mother was overwhelmed with all these kids and had no experience handling a large family to boot. They had no idea what my sister and brother had gone through. My new father's sons totally rejected my mother and basically hated her guts. As for me, my sister, and my baby brother—we hated everyone and ate like wild savages. These parents had stepped into a deep pile of set ablaze hot poo poo. They brought together all these kids from psycho dysfunction-vile without having a single clue what to do. And the cycle beats on. Dad was not a touchy-feely dad. He was very strict and "you need to fear him" is what he thought to be the answer. It merely became the fuel for more mental rage. He would rage, we would rage. He would put us on restriction. To us, that meant a challenge and we would stretch the rules to the max. We tested his resolve. He became more physical in his punishment [Not physically abusive]. We had the worst you can get; we were survivors of serious abuse.

I began to watch days turn into months and then years and begin to smarten up. I watched as, time after time, my brothers would brutally speak words of hate. They would defy their father and mother. I realized I did not want to cause any more pain, shame, or fear to my family. I stayed out of trouble as best as a curious boy could. I began focusing on how to help myself in this life. I went to church off and on. I was not really committed but interested in the girls, food, and fun. I began mowing grass and washing cars. It kept me busy and out of trouble. It even made my parents happy. I stuttered a little when I spoke and was extremely fearful of having to explain a mistake. I had no confidence in myself.

Years later, I could not fill out an employment application. It would take hours. I did not understand the questions they asked. I could not spell to save my life. As I got older, Dad filled out my application. I still did not understand what I was reading. Finally, we moved to Joplin, Missouri. I began working at a large newspaper route. Dad ended up paying money I had collected from customers and spent on candy. I was about twelve at this time. I acted like I was eighteen when I put good effort into it. I was still working odd jobs. I had gotten jobs like raking leaves and washing cars or anything I could sweat-talk my customer into. Like repairing or painting anything I could get my hands on. I was still in and out of churches.

We were moving again, this time to Las Vegas, Nevada. Seventh grade in Las Vegas was like being sent to prison every school day. I was sure someone was going to kill me just because I was slow to speak. All you had to say was boo, it would have made me pee my pants. Eighth grade was a little different. I guess I started getting better looking. I had a lot of attention from the girls. This made me pretty popular and a target for the local school gangs. Here is where I learned to put my hidden talent to work. I found out that fighting back meant respect. So, I began protecting myself and anyone who could not. It had gotten so bad my mother would have dreams about me getting jumped coming home from school. She called the school and asked me to walk home the long way. She was afraid I would come home with a bloody face. Sometimes I did.

High school quickly approached, and home life sucked big time. Our family had been torn to shreds by everyone. No one cared about anyone and every man for himself. I wanted to move out badly, but I had no car. My freshman year in high school was pretty smooth. I saw seniors roughing up freshmen all around me, but no one was pushing me around. Maybe I did not look like a freshman. I played football and was on the wrestling team. I always wanted Dad to come to my wrestling meets. He was also a wrestler in school. His schedule never allowed it. I also joined the choir and enjoyed it immensely. My sophomore year was just about the same.

I began to work a job full time. In my junior year, I did not go out for football or wrestling. I began to get bored with it. I was barely passing my classes during ninth and tenth grades. The eleventh grade quickly went by. This year, I got into smoking pot and drinking with friends. We would party all night long. I went to school and worked a full-time job. After work it was straight to the clubs to drink and dance. I was still a virgin and sex had begun to interest and terrify me. I still had been dealing with childhood fears. However, the subject terrified me. While at the clubs, I was approached by more men than ladies. That was different. I began to think maybe I was gay. Maybe everyone knows it but me? All my buddies were sleeping around (with ladies), and I just wanted to be friends with them. Unfortunately, I gave in. I lost my virginity to a one-night stand. She was very uninterested in me and never talked to me again. Twenty-two years later, when we bumped at a restaurant, she confessed to many years of sorrow for how she treated me and asked for forgiveness. She is now happily married.

After my fall with my one-night stand, I became angry. All I wanted to do was to find as many girls and ruin their lives. Regretfully, I became a jerk. Seek, conquer, and destroy. I was hateful and had plenty of it. Senior year came and parties were nonstop. My parents were generous enough to give me one of their cars, a big Pontiac Catalina. One of the best cars I have ever owned. Now I had wheels and freedom was now mine to take. I moved out of my parent's home. I was living with a girlfriend and her parents. At this time in my life, I was on a fast train to nowhere. First stop, HELL! What another very lost time in my life.

The school was a roller coaster ride. I missed so many days the principal threatened to not let me graduate! I had been invited to sing for a scholarship at UNIV. Right before graduation, I had won the scholarship. Things were looking up. My girlfriend's parents moved to a nearby town called Pahrump. In Vegas, we say over the hump in Pahrump. In Pahrump, I had gotten involved in shady dealings and almost got shot. I also never collected on the scholarship. I soon realized the path I was on was going to lead me straight to the grave or prison. I thought long and hard about my life. I was 18. I knew if I did not change my behavior, I would never make it alive.

I moved back to Las Vegas and met up with an old-school buddy. He was my best friend while we were in high school. He was a new believer in Christ and was active in his church. He happened to be dating a beautiful lady at the time and did not want me to meet her. I was renting a room from someone my best friend had introduced me to days earlier. Later, I found out the house belonged to my best friend's girlfriend's sister. Several weeks later, I was invited to a spaghetti dinner at the home I was renting a room from. My best friend was invited and unbeknown to him and me, his girlfriend was also invited. The moment she walked up the stairs, my eternity began. She was my dream come true. I see why he did not want me to meet her. Every word she spoke made me want to shout, I love you. I did not understand why he was so standoffish with her. I found out later they were separating. She was a peach, and I was in love at first sight. Yes, folks, it is true. Love does happen at first sight. After twenty years, I know it is true.

I moved in to get a closer look and she totally lifted her nose; she even rolled her eyes. She could not stand this arrogant and prideful dude. She was in her third year of college and I barely graduated high school. She was dating guys who had real cars. I owned a smoke bomb with rear explosions complimentary while slowing down to a stop sign. (I sold my Pontiac for a smaller car, a big mistake.) After a week of her niece's begs and pleads, her aunt decided to let her go out on a date. She finally gave into a double dare. Our first date was pretty fun until it came time to pay the bill. I forgot my wallet. I felt like I could just fall out of the chair and die. I had ordered a huge meal to try and impress my beautiful date. She was not happy about this. She had hardly touched her meal. I asked, is your food not good? She said, "Well, I do not eat meat and this lobster and steak smells weird?"

I nearly fell out of my seat. I actually began to choke on the bite I had taken. This put a serious strain on our first date. I was delirious by now. The waiter arrived and handed me the check. My eyes were instantly crossed. I could have sworn I was hallucinating. Not only was she not happy about the food, she was going to have to pay for this mess I got us in. Needless to say, the rest of the night was straight home. Did I mention she drove? It was so quiet in the car; you could hear the wear and tear coming off the tires. I just knew I would never see her again. I thought I better get my kiss before she drove away. (Hey, I never claimed to be the smartest person in the galaxy.)

As she was dropping me off at her sister's house (her sister's house, does that not sound redneck?), I decided this would be the moment to swoop in and get that kiss. I swooped in to give her a kiss. As I did, my eye caught the rear-view mirror and stopped me with a jolt. It felt like I had gotten hit in the eye with a baseball. I swung out of the door to regain my composure. I was so embarrassed. Within seconds, I thought of getting back in there, or she would drive off. So, swoop number two and again, my eye caught the rear-view mirror!! (No kidding, I was road kill by now. I stood there like a deer in the headlight look, in complete disarray.) Suddenly, I could hear her giggling so hard. I looked inside. She turned to me and said, "Please do not try that again. I will roll down my window so you can safely kiss me on the driver's side." Ya hoooo! One kiss was all it took for me to know she was the one. Soon after that date (I wore a bike helmet on our dates, just kidding?), we went on several dates. Our relationship caught fire.

Chapter 5: Quantum Faith

"I have learned, in whatsoever state I am, therewith to be content"
(Philippians 4:11).

"I went to America to convert the Indians; now who will convert me" (John
Wesley).

"Submission is the only reasoning between a creature and its maker and
contentment in his will is the best remedy we can apply to mis fortunes" (Sir
William Temple).

Welcome to "QUANTUM FAITH!" space, the final frontier. To explore new places, to boldly go where no man has gone before!!! Sounds very familiar to Star Trek fans. Yes, I am one too. Love to watch space flicks. Let me tell you the definition of quantum faith in Nazarene terms. Quantum faith is the smallest quantity of energy we call hope. The very size of a mustard seed. Quantum faith has three sides:

1. Warfare 2. Welfare 3. Love affair

Warfare is defined as struggle and/or strife. As a believer, you are no stranger to the struggle and/or strife of this life. Praise our King; we are allowed to lay it down at his feet. As you are quite familiar with Eph 6:12, "For our struggle is not against flesh and blood, but against the rulers, against the authorities, against the powers of this dark world and against the spiritual forces of evil in the heavenly realms." We are talking serious warfare. Your faith must be built up to stand the constant barrage of lies. Your faith must be strong enough to fight the taunting of your sinful desires. Listen, this Devil has been around since time on Earth began. He (or she) has studied every move man has made and has capitalized on our fleshly sadness. Oftentimes, his standard mode of operation is to get you addicted and watch you dig your own pit and fall right in.

Going to war takes strict training and your new posture of combat faith to be your first response. Soldiers are taught to repeat instruction until they can say it in their sleep. The purpose of this routine is to cause a soldier to react to extreme situations without thinking about his actions. A soldier drills and drills his response, so it becomes his second nature. Therefore, he is trained with automatic reflexes. Soldiers do not panic because their training becomes their second nature, an automatic reflection. "For physical training is of some value, but godliness has value for all things, holding promise for both the present and the life to come" (1 Timothy 4:8). "Set your mind on things above, not on earthly things" (Colossians 3:1) Their comfort level reflects how much faith they have in their training. The harder you train yourself, the greater your faith reflects your strength in Christ. I have heard countless testimonies of combat soldiers having lived through grenade attacks, sniper fire, hand-to-hand combat, and IED (Improvised Explosive Devise) landmine explosions. All stories ended with: I should have been dead. Why me? Why did I not get hit? Why did I survive and no one else? This is a classic example of walking in quantum time. (Time, in this instance, is just an illusion.)

Our existence and the longevity of our existence has nothing to do with luck; it is fate. God holds all things, works all things, and creates all things for His glory. Jesus is the author of life and death. Life and death submit to Christ in all situations. Grace and gravity are both synonymous. They are both invisible and irresistible. Either one of them requires your belief in their existence. They have existed in a constant form. While even when the earth was formless it held water upon itself. That is pure evidence of gravitational existence. We who believe must hold to unshakable faith. A faith that says no matter the price, I will move forward no matter the cost. This faith moves in a realm of time no one can identify or see with the naked eye. Only with the eyes of faith can we believe. We understand quantum faith in warfare to be a reality. Survival does not always mean the faithful or non-faith will survive? "He causes his sun to rise on the evil and the good, and sends rain on the righteous and the unrighteous" (Matthew 5:45). God's will is what makes quantum existence amazing for all those who believe and do not believe.

Welfare, on the other hand, has an amazing quantum standard. It is similar to warfare through faith. This faith also moves in the realm of quantum faith with a different equation when considering God's will for our lives. Allow me to explain. "The Lord will grant you abundant prosperity" (Deuteronomy 28:11). "If you fully obey the Lord your God your God and carefully follow all His commands" (Deuteronomy 28:1). Not a life of sinlessness. Who lives a perfect life? Only the Lord can do that. In many Christian circles, we hear the ever-piercing question, "I wish I knew God's will for my life?" We have an amazing God and King. He requires our obedience in complete faithfulness and truth. He examines our every move and attitude. He is not some angry God ready to pounce on you when you mess up. He does not want to squash you like some bug on the sidewalk. He examines the heart and aligns the attitude. He will see if you measure up to your word. He does not record all your wrongs. You are saved by grace through faith.

A good friend of mine once said, "We need to be one with our word as Christ is one with His word." Thanks, Ray. That is a statement worthy of repeating to yourself. As you read this commentary, I really want you to see God's will for your life and mine. You have read in your Bible that if we love Him, we will obey Him. There is a mega problem in our understanding of His will and our will. He has put us in charge of this earth and everything in it from the beginning. Have we been good stewards, or are we still in the what is God's will for my life, stage? I know you have read in God's Word, "If a man will not work, he shall not eat" (2 Thessalonians 3:10). This scripture helps us to see God has given us the freedom to make up our own mind. He still loves us if we work or not. We are in charge of our day; he directs our feet. Our faith is God's welfare through our responsibility to obey His Word. We are to be wise in our decision-making process.

Quantum faith is knowing we walk and talk with an awesome creator. He has given us permission to be really transparent with Him. This does not give us a license to sin; God's grace is not a place to wipe our feet. Stop looking for God's will. It is right here in His word. "If you love me, you will obey what I command" (John 14:15). Furthermore, "Be joyful always; pray continually; give thanks in all circumstances, for this is God's will for you in Christ Jesus" (1 Thessalonians 5:16-18). God's will is all about His decrees and standards, not what you are supposed to do with your life. Take charge of the small time you have in existence. Do not sin on purpose; deny yourself and pick up the cross. That is a visual command. You would rather pick up the cross than cross into darkness for more pleasure. When you sin sexually, you sin against your own flesh. (1 Corinthians 6:18) Then you trash your witness to Christ. When you sin otherwise, you sin against your brother, sister, and your witness to Christ publicly. When you have denied Christ, you have sinned against the Cross of Christ. Then you sin against humanity, which God, your creator, has established. Make decisions and follow through for the sake of the cross. Period!

Every decision had better be made with the truth of God's word. It is all about your heart. It is not about what you decide. It is why. Is it about your pride or the guiding of the Holy Spirit tempering your understanding? Is your decision an extreme testimony for the whole world to witness? You are not of this world; you are not your former person. "Do not conform any longer to the patterns of this world, but be transformed by the renewing of your mind. Then you will be able to test and approve what God's will is—his good, pleasing and perfect will" (Romans 12:2). You have the liberty to function in your personality. You need to be faithful and true. Our welfare functions in a quantum knowledge of God's perfect will as a result of our obedience to his word of grace. God clothed himself in the flesh. He became lower than the angles and equal to man. He began an eternal love affair of the heart.

This is my third point: love affair. Weigh carefully His sacrifice for you. Weigh carefully when determining how you live in public and in private. I do not have the slightest notion of how God might have felt when He created man. God is omniscient presence and His power is overwhelming. I have an opportunity to talk with the homeless often. I know I did not create the homeless person. I could never account for God's view of the creator, looking into the eyes of my creation by any means. Let us just say, a very small inclination. As I have spoken to this person, I realize just how articulate and spirited my own personality is. I am well dressed. I am clean as a whistle, to boot. I could out-think this person in a quantum second. I could probably maneuver with extreme skill before he could even recognize I had even left my position. Man, does this not sound incredibly arrogant and self-righteous? You bet it does. Once in a while, I hang around the homeless. I understand them better when I become associated with their existence. I come down to their level like Christ came down to our level. As a soldier, I will give up my life for a homeless person as if they were my neighbor. Christ died for you and me when we were homeless. He died for us when we rejected him (Heaven is our home now). God could have been disastrous, but yet he postured himself in a sincere love beyond our feeble thinking. We have a love affair with awesome God. "Love must be sincere. Hate what is evil; cling to what is good. Be devoted to one another in brotherly love. Honor one another above yourself. Never be lacking in zeal, but keep your spiritual fervor, serving the Lord. Be joyful in hope, patient in affliction, faithful in prayer. Share with God's people who are in need. [Poor and homeless] Practice hospitality. Bless those who persecute you; bless and do not curse. Rejoice with those who rejoice; mourn with those who mourn. Live in harmony with one another. Do not be proud, but be willing to associate with people of low position. Do not be conceited. Do not repay anyone evil for evil. Be careful to do what is right in the eye of everybody. If it is possible, as far as it depends on you, live at peace with everyone. Do not take advantage, my friends, but leave room for God's wrath, for it is written: 'It is mine to avenge; I will repay," says the Lord. On the contrary: "If your enemy is hungry, feed him; if he is thirsty; give him something to drink. In doing this, you will heap burning coals on his head. Do not be overcome by evil, but overcome evil with good" (Romans 12:9- 21).

Thank you for reading this heart-to-heart message. May the Lord, our God, bless you always and all you set your heart upon. Be joyful, be serious for Jesus and leave room for mistakes. March with a new sense of pride in Christ. You are meant to position yourself in Christ, believe his grace is freedom, and walk with a uniform faith in the United Saints Nazarene Core as a Nazarene soldier. We are the "Extreme Nazarenes!"

Example of Church Structure for the United Saint Nazarene Corp.

Christian Legislator
The Congress of Christ

Commander and Chief
JESUS CHRIST

Bi-lateral congress
President—Senior Pastor
Vice Pres—Exe. Senior Assoc. Pastor
House Speaker Senior Exe. Pastor

BICAMERAL
Legislation

Senators—Sen. Exe. Pastor
Council of Elders
Appointed Pastors
Upper house of legislation
(ministry leaders)

Congressmen—Board
members
Office of Deacons
Elected Officers and
Administrator
Lower house of legislation

Definition of positions
Governing body
Respect
Godly Reverence respect

Definition of position
Legislative (Make and Enact
laws)
Honorable

Senatorial Seating
Assoc. Pastors

Armor bearers
Congregational house of rep
Ministry Supervisors

Senate Floor
Lay Pastors
Administrate (Manages)

Definition of position
Respect: Highly regarded

(Voluntary) Administers
(Executive) Altar Captains
Delegate's (Trusted)
Definition of position
Respect: Eminently Respected
Definition of position
Respect: Noble

Floor Congressional
Employed Professionals
Ministry Leaders (Voluntary)
Mission Capable (Proven)

Definition of position
Respect: Worthy

Introduction to the EXTREME NAZARENE "United Saints Nazarene Corp."

Hello, my name is Adam Childress. I would like to take some time to tell you about the USNC (United Saints Nazarene Corps—The Extreme Nazarenes). As you know, Jesus Christ is the ultimate Extreme Nazarene. He is our supreme commander and chief. Nazarenes are men and women who believe that Jesus Christ is Lord of all. We believe that our battle is not against flesh and blood but against the rulers, against the authorities, against the powers of this dark world, and against the spiritual forces of evil in the heavenly realms (Ephesians 6-12).

As United Saints Nazarene soldiers, we are commissioned to tell everyone about the saving grace of Jesus Christ. As a US Nazarene, you are required by God's word to be "Faithful and True," our motto (Revelations 19:11). We consider ourselves to be powerful soldiers for Christ. Powerful means we lead the way in speech, in life, in love, in faith and in purity (1 Timothy 4:12). Forceful men lay hold of the kingdom of heaven (Matthew 11:12). We Are soldiers with spiritual courage, vigor, power, and determination because of ever-present persecution.

We are dedicated to the obedience of Christ and honor His saving grace with our lives. We do not surrender. Nazarene personnel must be actively participating in a local Christian church, Bible fellowship, and home group. You will not meet anyone like a Nazarene soldier in the USNC.

Furthermore, Nazarenes are soldiers who have caught the vision of being active in the most powerful Christian Military Spiritual Corp on the planet ever. Some soldiers who have been in the active-duty military are bringing their experience and training to the Nazarene Corp as civilians. I have been a strong believer that once a soldier, always a soldier. Nothing can take that away from you. Those of you who are military minded will also enjoy being an active-duty servant soldier. Join us and learn the way of the Extreme Nazarene.

God, our father, is always looking for a few faithful and true soldiers. As an ex-military person, I can tell you I miss the camaraderie of fellow soldiers. Persons you know without a doubt, will be there for you. They will even lay down their life for you. We are extreme! That is the kind of extreme love our Savior died for. Jesus battled sin for you and me. He surrendered to the Cross on Calvary for us. We must never forget the price He paid for our freedom from hell! We must never forget the price our forefathers paid for our liberties as they followed Christ's example of sacrifice for our way of life in America today. Unfortunately, America has forgotten her principles of God's amazing grace.

We will battle sin moment by moment. We will call our fellow soldiers' unquenchable thirst for our blood before we fall into sins. (Call before you fall!) It works, too. We are elite Christian fighting warriors. We are the warriors of the light. It is time to soldier up. The battle rages and the time is at hand. We need to stand so that when the day of evil comes, we may be able to stand our ground.

We all have our own responsibilities in this life, but we do not have to face life's battles on our own. Are you tired of the enemy ambush? Have you had enough? Did you surrender? Have you been taken as a POW long enough? Do you need a rescue team to get you out? It is time to get a fellow combat soldier to endure during your tour of duty. There are too many Christian MIAs. We need to be on the front lines, saving lives in the name of Jesus Christ. It is time to go door to door with the Gospel of Christ.

Let us know when you are ready to become an Extreme Nazarene. Go to www.unitedsaintsnazarenecorp.com

Adam P. Childress
US Nazarene Corp. Commanding

What is a Nazarene?

A Nazarene is a man or woman who has a call by Christ, our King, to obey His word, uphold His truths and lay down his or her life for the defenseless.

A Nazarene is a present-day saint, a hero of the faith.

A Nazarene is a person who rescues people in physical harm.

A Nazarene is someone who upholds the laws of the land, here or abroad.

A Nazarene is always defending Christ, family, church, neighbor, stranger, country, and freedom.

A Nazarene is always teaching, learning, loving, living, and obeying God's word for themselves and others.

A Nazarene always sets the example in speech, faith, life, love, and purity (1 Tim 4:12).

A Nazarene is constantly training him or herself to be Godly in all things (1 Tim 4:07).

Who can be a Nazarene?

Any person who has been born again. Anyone who has lived a life approved by Christian people can account for their lifestyle. Persons who have been involved in commissioning through their local church. Persons who have been ordained and/or licensed in ministry to preach the Gospel of Jesus Christ.

Nazarene Company Foundation

Ten reasons why we participate in Christian soldiery:

1) Commitment and Leadership to preserve our nation's principles.
2) To step up and make serving their neighbor a priority.
3) Return to the fellowship of the saints of all ages.
4) Discipleship and effective communication.
5) Strengthen the group through prayer and fasting.
6) Learn and teach accountability.
7) Connect our lives to all believers around the world.
8) To know you have a true soldier watching yourback (meet a combat buddy).
9) Help discover people's gifts and talents.
10) Support fatherhood and motherhood.

Nazarene Vision

1) Neighborhood Evangelism.
2) Team Building.
3) Mentor parents to be godly dads and moms.

4) Measuring up as men and women of integrity.

5) We are the offspring of the royal family of Christ.

6) Nazarene means protector or guardian of absolutetruth.

7) Consecrated means to be dedicated to the sacredservice of Christ.

Book and Scripture References

All scripture quotes are from the "Concordia Self-study Bible" NIV. All scripture quotes with author intent are marked with the following: [sample]

All commentary quotes come from the "Concordia Self-study Bible" NIV.

Author Steve Farrar

Book reference: Pointman

Pastor Paul Palmer Sermon Notes and Quotes:

Vista New Life Church, El Paso, TX, 1988

Practical ways to guard against impurities: 1. Be consistent in my communion with God. 2. Appropriate by faith our deliverance from sin. 3. Be accountable to a pastor or mature friend. 4. Keep as a priority in marriage communication and romance. 5. Rehearse regularly the consequences of adultery. 6. Break off any associations where you are likely to be tempted. 7. Be honest with yourself and God; recognize vulnerable areas. The enemy maximizes the pleasure and minimizes the consequences. Qualities of a velvet man: 1. A man who cares; gives his family presence, not presents; kids spell love time. 2. A man of consideration; he listens to others needs and feelings; compassionate. 3. A man of conduct, he is courteous, gentle man. Qualities of a man of steel: 1. Committed-an activator, not responder. 2. Conviction-studies and lives by the bible regardless of what society says. 3. Courage-stands up for what's right in the face of opposition. 4. Control-disciplined, allows the fruit of the spirit to grow and cultivates it.

Pitfalls for us as men: 1. Position, prosperity,and purity. 2. Might, money and morals. 3. Girls, gold and glory. A relationship with God: 1. Intimacy requires holiness, holiness requires humility, humility requires teachableness, teachableness requires thankfulness, thankfulness requires a listening ear. Roles in the home for the father: 1. Priest-I represent my family to God. 2. Prophet-I speak the word of God to my family. 3. King-I govern my family for God. Quote: Sow a thought, reap an act: sow an act reap ahabit, sow a habit, reap a character, sow a character reap a destiny.

Pastor Mike Richardson
International Church of Las Vegas, NV, 2002
Quote: Not on my watch.

Pastor Paul Goulet
International Church of Las Vegas, NV, 1999
Quote: Christer's (Christmas and Easter).
ABC's of faithconfession.

Pastor C.J. Mahaney
Sovereign Grace Ministries
Quote: Church dress attire

Author Friedrich Rest
Book Reference: Our Christian Symbols

Department of Veteran Affairs Website
Definition: Post Traumatic Stress Disorder

Author John Eldredge

Book Reference: Wild at Heart

National Geomagnetic Information Center Website

Definition: Map reading and True North

My DNA.com Website

Symptoms of bipolar disorder.

Acknowledgments

Jesus Christ—My Master, Savior, and Commander

Sawyer, Metzger, Trent, and Petit—Love to laugh together

Dolores Brown—You trusted me with your daughter

Chaplain Dan—You let me preach in the Gulf

Paul Goulet—My pastor and teacher

Mark & Christine McLoone-We are as one

Mike Richardson—My mentor and friend

John Mazur—A virtual warrior

Bayles, Williams, Hohenstein and Cadicamo—Awesome fellowship

Twenty years of wonderful family friendship and ministry